AF827076

Monetary Policy Instruments
for European Monetary Union

Springer
Berlin
Heidelberg
New York
Barcelona
Budapest
Hong Kong
London
Milan
Paris
Santa Clara
Singapore
Tokyo

Lukas Menkhoff

Monetary Policy Instruments for European Monetary Union

With 8 Figures
and 16 Tables

Springer

Prof. Dr. Lukas Menkhoff
Aachen University of Technology
Department of Economics
D-52056 Aachen
Germany

We kindly thank Deutscher Sparkassenverlag GmbH, Stuttgart for granting permission to publish the English version of Geldpolitische Instrumente der Europäischen Zentralbank.

Cataloging-in-Publication Data applied for
Die Deutsche Bibliothek - CIP-Einheitsaufnahme

Menkhoff, Lukas:
Monetary policy instruments for European monetary union : mit 16 Tabellen / Lukas Menkhoff. - Berlin ; Heidelberg ; New York ; Barcelona ; Budapest ; Hongkong ; London ; Mailand ; Paris ; Santa Clara ; Singapur ; Tokio : Springer, 1997
ISBN 3-540-62454-6

ISBN 3-540-62454-6 Springer-Verlag Berlin Heidelberg New York

This work is subject to copyright. All rights are reserved, whether the whole or part of the material is concerned, specifically the rights of translation, reprinting, reuse of illustrations, recitation, broadcasting, reproduction on microfilm or in any other way, and storage in data banks. Duplication of this publication or parts thereof is permitted only under the provisions of the German Copyright Law of September 9, 1965, in its current version, and permission for use must always be obtained from Springer-Verlag. Violations are liable for prosecution under the German Copyright Law.

© Springer-Verlag Berlin · Heidelberg 1997
Printed in Germany

The use of general descriptive names, registered names, trademarks, etc. in this publication does not imply, even in the absence of a specific statement, that such names are exempt from the relevant protective laws and regulations and therefore free for general use.

SPIN 10566325 42/2202-5 4 3 2 1 0 – Printed on acid-free paper

Foreword

This book represents the revised and enlarged results of a research project which recieved financial support from the "Wissenschaftsförderung der Sparkassenorganisation e.V." and was originally published in German (Menkhoff 1996). As the issue of monetary policy instruments for EMU is one which is inherently international, the publication of an English edition is a logical step. I whish to thank the Deutscher Sparkassenverlag, which published the German edition, for encouraging work on this subsequent project.

The major innovation in the English edition is the inclusion of several new sections, i.e. 3.2.4, 3.3.4, 3.3.5, 3.4.3 and 3.5. These new analyses, together with changing institutional circumstances and the addition of new literature have also resulted in a large number of minor changes throughout the text.

The book is a contribution, from a German perspective, to the discussion about monetary policy instruments of the future European Central Bank. The main instruments are analyzed from the point of view of efficiency; in addition, the need to harmonize often divergent sets of national policy instruments means that an emphasis on the additional goal of fair competition is of particular relevance. Last but not least, the explicit linking of EMU to the concept of subsidiarity has wide-ranging consequences for monetary policy instruments.

I would like to express my gratitude to Axel Bertuch-Samuels, Bernd Braasch, Heinz Herrmann, Jürgen Jerger, Eberhart Ketzel, Klaus Krummrich, Norbert Tolksdorf and Hans-Jürgen Treutler for their helpful advice and comments during the course of writing and revising the book. I would also like to thank the participants at the 1995 CEPR/Irving Fisher Society-Conference on "What Monetary Policy for the European Central Bank?"

and the 1996 conference on "European Monetary Union: Transition, International Impacts and Policy Options" of the European Institution for International Economic Relations for their constructive discussions.

Finally, my particular thanks go to Robin Bonthrone for his excellent translation (additional material by the author), to Catherine Plitzko for her invaluable lay-out assistance and again to the "Wissenschaftsförderung" for its financial support.

Aachen, November 1996 Lukas Menkhoff

Contents

1 Introduction

1.1 The problems

The creation of a new European System of Central Banks (ESCB), headed by a European Central Bank (ECB), raises the question of the instruments of monetary policy which will be used by these institutions. With no homogeneity in the array of instruments employed across Europe today, there can certainly be no automatic solution to this problem, as various traditions are now competing head-on in this field.

These traditions are of much more than marginal significance, reflecting the fundamental concepts of how national institutions, and thus European institutions - including the ECB - should function. In line with its own federal structure, the German position in this competitive arena tends to support decentralized decision-making structures, competition between differing organizational forms and the principle of subsidiarity. Even where other countries fundamentally approve of these principles, implementation in concrete terms may well lead to divergent views on how this should be achieved, as these will be based almost inevitably on the countries' own established structures.

Although this interest in the future arrangements for the monetary policy instruments of the ECB - and the ECB will also be taken as representative of all the national central banks (ESCB) in this study - affects all the countries involved to an equal extent, an additional concern is evident for those countries tending towards decentralized organizational structures. Contrary to the declared beliefs in institutional diversity, subsidiarity and decentralized structures, it is likely from the outset that the shift in responsibility for monetary policy from the nation states to the European level will be accompanied by more uniform policy instruments and greater centralization in their employment.

On the other hand, however, it should not be assumed automatically that Germany's existing monetary policy instruments would necessarily be the best for the ECB, just because they happen to have demonstrated their usefulness in the past. This study will therefore examine in detail the potential instruments of monetary policy open to the ECB. Emphasis will be placed on fair competition and decentralization, firstly because these aspects are expected to result in substantial divisions between the countries involved, and secondly because they are of particular interest to Germany, for the reasons outlined above. However, a strict requirement for any discussion is, of course, that the monetary efficiency of the instruments is ensured.

The tasks involved in this study can therefore be summarized as an analysis of the instruments of the ECB to establish

- how efficient they are in terms of monetary policy,
- the extent to which they distort competition between various organizational forms and
- in case of doubt, whether they tend to promote rather than discriminate against decentralized organizations and decision-making structures, in line with the principle of subsidiarity.

To allow concentration on the core problems, the monetary policy instruments in this study have been restricted from the outset to minimum reserve, open market and refinancing policies, as these represent the most important instruments at national level. In particular, the balance of payments issues which do not fall under the remit of the ECB - such as any decision on the exchange rate system - have been essentially ignored, in addition to those with effects similar to domestic instruments, above all open market policy.

Wherever possible, the analysis will only focus on key aspects relating to the market participants affected and the more detailed design of specific instruments. The spotlight will be on the dominant commercial banks, with non-banks, building societies and so on being disregarded.

Another topic which has been limited is the notion of decentralization. In principle, monetary policy can also be viewed as an instrument of regional policy, for instance when the subsidy components of a low-interest discount policy are selectively channelled into economically disadvantaged regions. However, financial policy considerations in particular mean that this interpretation of the tasks of monetary policy has no appreciable advocates: if the objective of monetary policy - monetary stability - were to be watered down by competing goals, its primary function could be violated (see Lehment/Scheide, 1992). Moreover, a range of other regional or structural policy options is available, and the aspect of recognizable responsibility dictates that instruments should be geared to a single goal wherever possible.

Finally, the monetary policy instruments will generally be analysed in isolation from specific monetary strategies, intermediate targets or indicators. There are certainly a number of interdependencies, but this approach appears justified in order to provide a clear and understandable overview. It may, however, be helpful to view this examination of monetary policy instruments as being based on the Bundesbank concept.

1.2 The background to the goals of the study

The previous section highlighted three aspects around which the examination of the monetary policy instruments of the ECB will be based. The definition of these aspects has been derived from particular interests and to this extent, it sets a standard for the entire study. For this reason, mention will be made throughout of three "goals" against which the instruments will be measured. This section examines the background to these goals in greater detail.

There is basically no alternative to setting such prescriptive goals. Even confining the study to the ostensibly "neutral" aspect of efficiency would simply mask out other goals without any justification for such a course at a prescriptive level. On the other hand, other goals could also be discussed, such as the regional support policies already excluded, or explicit preferential treatment for existing or target market structures. Although any definition of the goals will necessarily remain arbitrary to a minor extent, the goals of "efficiency", "fair competition" and "decentralization" pursued in this study can still be derived more convincingly than any purely subjective choice.[1]

This will probably hold true for monetary efficiency more than any other goal, but this merely means that the defined function of monetary policy will be achieved most simply using the instruments at hand. In this respect, cost efficiency is also a secondary component of the goal of monetary efficiency.

---

[1] These same considerations are expressed in different terms by the Deutsche Bundesbank, 1992, p. 90; Remsperger's "principles" can also be classified in similar fashion, see Remsperger, 1994, p. 261.

The notion of fair competition is linked to the prescriptive concept of an appropriate degree of government intervention in the life of the economy. The German concept is that the state generally provides a functioning environment for private economic activity, within which competition ensures that demand is satisfied efficiently. In terms of monetary policy, this means that state regulation of the size, organizational form, location and business structure of credit institutions is limited. Exceptions to this are, for example, minimum capital adequacy requirements, restrictions on types of operation or balance sheet structure directives. This study does not attempt to call into question this existing regulatory framework. Fair competition merely implies that the employment of monetary policy instruments should not cause any additional distortion of competition between the credit institutions. However, it should be noted that unavoidable regulation may well be at odds with the principle of fair competition to a certain extent: "The idea that Central Banks should concentrate on the aggregates, and ignore the development of the constituent parts, and the structure of the financial system, is alien to the historical record" (Goodhart, 1992, p. 23)

The goal of fair competition will inevitably meet its limits where monetary efficiency is affected. In borderline cases, one can imagine a shift on the financial markets to which an efficient monetary policy can react faster than some competitors. This means that fair competition cannot be a "guardian angel" for existing competitors or forms of credit institution. In such cases, monetary policy would act as a brake on market-driven structural change. On the other hand, neither should this concept of monetary policy be any sort of "industrial policy" which actively identifies institutions regarded as competitive and either encourages them, or treats them differently than others.

The goal of decentralization is defined by an overriding political objective. The European Union has adopted the fundamental principle of subsidiarity, under which decisions should be taken at the organisational level closest to its citizens, wherever this is feasible. In this respect, decentralization is not an unconditional, but a conditional goal, i.e. there should only be a departure from subsidiarity, or in this case decentralization, if this is necessary for reasons of efficiency.

This final restriction affecting achievement of the goal of decentralization highlights a potential conflict between the three goals which must somehow be solved. In essence, this assumes the existence of a goal hierarchy which emerges if fair competition and decentralization are interpreted as conditional goals. Over and above this, however, there is still an area where there is no "scientific" imperative about the optimum instruments to use, but rather where the economic consequences of various options become apparent.

1.3 The structure of the study

Before moving on to the essence of this study - an analysis of the instruments in terms of the three defined goals - in Chapter Three, a number of fundamental issues must first be addressed.

The second chapter on the instruments of monetary policy of the ECB will therefore examine the status quo and potential future directions, since these factors will define the framework within which monetary policy instruments must be integrated and used. The basic money provisioning alternatives will be outlined together with their implications in some European countries. This analysis of the underlying options, the legal framework and longitudinal and cross-sectional trends will then produce an initial overview on consensus and controversy in Europe.

Chapter Three forms the core of the study, containing an analysis of potential instruments in terms of the three goals described above. As far as structuring this examination is concerned, it would be convenient to analyse efficiency initially by assuming an "optimum" environment, in particular by ignoring information problems and externalities. It is immediately obvious that such a reduction in the degree of complexity can result in the use of a comparatively simple range of instruments, above all open market policy.

A number of specific problems will then be introduced into this simplified approach, and logically enough, these will have implications for the efficient organization of monetary policy instruments. The reason behind this approach is to base minimum reserve and refinancing policies on specific breaches of the simplified initial scenario. The more traditional pro and contra arguments about the two instruments will be reinforced by a more detailed discussion of a relatively new concept for justifying refinancing policy: to shield the real economy from interference originating from the financial sector.

The case for the three key instruments of monetary policy will also be discussed in relation to fair competition. In addition, attention will be given to proposals for reforming the relatively problematic minimum reserve and refinancing policies aimed at eliminating the distortions produced by these instruments almost completely. It is these proposed reforms which make a more detailed study of the - otherwise relatively minor - competition problems of open market policies an interesting subject.

Finally, monetary policy instruments will be analysed in terms of the goal of decentralization. At least three aspects are important in this context: decentralization in the financial sector, implications of idiosyncratic financing structures and decentralization in the organization of the ECB itself. As far as Germany is concerned, the issue of decentralization in the financial sector can be narrowed down to those structures worth retaining, such as the size of the institutions, locations and organizational forms. Regarding national differences in financing structures, these may influence the transmission of monetary policy stimuli and thus encourage some decentralized policy elements. In terms of the central bank, decentralization relates to both the organizational structure and the workflows in the process of implementing monetary policy.

Chapter Four will then discuss and assess alternative proposals - i.e. grouping together various instruments oriented towards specific characteristics - on the basis of these analyses. To limit the scope of the discussion, an almost certain minimum consensus among the decision-makers on what action should be taken will be assumed. This will then be used as the basis of three fundamental concepts for monetary policy instruments: a "lean", a "conservative" and a "decentralized" concept. As the first two concepts are comparatively well-known, the third will be explained in greater detail. In doing so, the fundamental concept can be split away from specific design proposals, on which further empirical work must be done.

Finally, this is followed by a brief conclusion to the study in Chapter Five.

2 The monetary policy instruments of the European Central Bank

2.1 Restricting the subject

Although it is possible in theory to conceive entirely new monetary policy instruments for the ECB, or for the ESCB overall, practical reasons dictate that such a complete redesign is somewhat unlikely, as numerous instruments already exist in the Member States of the European Union. Indeed, a total innovation would probably be a pointless exercise, as it would involve a substantial degree of uncertainty about the way in which specific instruments would or could function, a consequence which can be avoided by building on existing arrangements. The intrinsic value of continuity and stability as key economic policy factors is particularly critical for the sensitive financial markets.

However, a fundamental question to be answered is that of the overall framework within which monetary policy instruments are decided.

- This framework is headed by the binding legal agreements to be found in the treaties on Economic and Monetary Union. Even if the treaties are modified at some time, a procedure advocated by some observers, these notions are geared to tightening the convergence criteria (e.g. Jochimsen, 1994) or aimed at establishing a "competitive model" between national central banks, although this model features identical monetary policy instruments (e.g. Willeke, 1994).
- The second basis for considering the ECB's instruments of monetary policy could be existing trends which provide at least a rough direction for the discussion. At any rate, a longitudinal analysis would be useful if it is assumed that these trends are tightly bound up with

the characteristics of the existing financial systems. At the same time, this heightens awareness of the historical, i.e. institution-driven design of monetary policy instruments.
- The third and final starting point is a cross-sectional analysis of the current arrangements in key countries. An underlying assumption for such an analysis is that all existing instruments are fundamentally efficient. Such a comparative analysis can then draw attention both to the differences identified, and to the related question of the extent to which they are the result of institutional or monetary policy orientation, as well as the room for manoeuvre they offer.

Before analysing the consequences of the three approaches - in the order described above - for the range of probable options for monetary policy instruments, Chapter 2.2 will take a look at a number of simple theoretical principles.

2.2 Monetary policy instruments

Although the ultimate objective of using monetary policy instruments is to influence the activities of the target players in the economy, this goal is mostly achieved indirectly in a market economy. As a rule, the central bank brings its influence to bear on the commercial banks by controlling the provision of central bank money. In simple terms, it can determine creation or usage (see Ehrlicher, 1973). Because the term "usage" can also hint at a structural component - in the sense of a structure of uses - one could also speak of linkage and "destruction" (Issing, 1993, p. 63).

The credit allocation structure can also be influenced directly, or the volume of credit restricted, but this does not correspond to the modern concept of monetary policy. These more interventionist ideas are dismissed because they could "open the door" to unlimited demands on monetary policy. In particular, this can turn minds to the conflict between a strict policy of price stability, and short-term moves towards easing monetary policy to stimulate the economy.

Furthermore, *Ordnungspolitik* considerations alone are bound to cause unease about quantitative or sectoral control measures.[1]

[1] *Ordnungspolitik* refers to a view of economic policy which is popular and influential in Germany. It stresses the importance of setting an appropriate (regulatory) framework for private economic activities.

To return to the monetary policy basis of the creation and usage of central bank money, a distinction is made between four different triggers for creation (see Issing/Rudolph, 1988, pp. 12 ff.):

- a balance of payments component,
- an open market component,
- a refinancing component
- and a fiscal component.

Assuming the case of the creation of central bank money, the latter typically buys foreign currency from commercial banks (the balance of payments component) and provides central bank money in exchange. In the case of the open market component, the central bank will buy short-term securities (money market paper), with the central bank taking the initiative. Refinancing operations in Germany are normally based on bills, with the commercial bank taking the initiative. And finally in the case of the fiscal component, the central bank extends credit to the government, typically by buying government securities.

By distinguishing between these four exhaustive components of central bank money creation, monetary policy instruments can be allocated accordingly. However, there is a need for further information in the case of the fiscal component, because open market operations are also based, as a rule, on government securities. However, credit is then extended to the government indirectly through the commercial bank intermediaries. More revealingly, there is no incentive or even obligation for the central bank to actively support the government. The government is the incidental, rather than the intentional beneficiary of monetary policy, which considerably strengthens the central bank's position.

Moreover, the refinancing policy can be implemented using securities, which is why this term is sometimes used as a generic term for open market and refinancing policy in the narrower sense. This applies, for example, to lombard loans backed by a pledge of securities. In this respect, attention should be paid not only to the underlying securities of the monetary policy instruments, but also to the "initiator" of the relevant measures, when making a distinction between open market and refinancing policy. As a general rule, refinancing policy contains an elastic component of central bank money provision, i.e. the initiative to create money comes from the commercial banks within a framework deliberately created by the central bank.

The prime instrument on the usage side is that of minimum reserve requirement policy, under which commercial banks are required to maintain deposits at the central bank as a fixed ratio of their on-balance sheet business. The reserve requirement ratios are typically based on the bank's liabilities. As a rule, the more near-liquid forms of deposit are subject to higher ratios.

Apart from these five key categories of monetary policy instruments, whose organization may differ considerably from the outlines given above in specific instances, there is a wide range of other measures whose importance does not approach that of the instruments already described. Some of these are measures oriented towards the balance of payments, whilst others are fine-tuning measures.[2]

The instruments geared to the balance of payments are designed to control capital movements. Examples of these are special minimum reserve requirements for non-residents, fiscal regulations for foreign currency transactions or direct restrictions on capital movements. As a rule, however, the powers to enforce these types of measures are vested with the national governments rather than the central banks, even when the latter are consulted and must themselves employ the instruments.

As regards fine-tuning measures, the name itself denotes that these are not the quantitative backbone of monetary policy management. However, this does not mean that they are necessarily marginal if they are important for communication between the central bank and the markets. This applies, for instance, to several smaller measures used by the Bundesbank for selective market influence. In terms of the organization of the instruments, however, they are largely comparable to open market transactions.

The final part of this section will show how the instruments of monetary policy are reflected in the balance sheet of a central bank, in this case the Bundesbank. Using the criterion of the ability to manage balance sheet items, a distinction is made between core and marginal monetary policy measures, as well as a third group of balance sheet items lying outside these measures.

In the current situation at the Bundesbank, the marginal activities principally comprise items related to the balance of payments, because these can remain unchanged when exchange rates are flexible, in other words they are of little importance to monetary policy. In the EMS, with its narrower bands, intervention obligations are a matter for the two central banks affected, at least in theory. In practice, however, intramarginal intervention predominates, i.e. the central banks representing weak currencies - which rarely count the D-mark among their number - act

---

[2] For a more detailed elaboration on the German case see Issing, 1993, pp. 114 ff. or Deutsche Bundesbank, 1995.

alone in the events leading up to mandatory bilateral intervention, with a result that the Bundesbank infrequently has to take any action. In such a situation, currency reserves are basically a sort of emergency instrument which is deployed if flexible exchange rates move well outside the parities regarded as reasonable.

The simplified Bundesbank balance sheet at the end of February 1996 (*Table 1*) shows that assets are dominated by the "core" activities, whilst equity and liabilities are driven by non-manageable activities, this situation being due to the weighting of notes in circulation in relation to the balance sheet total. Adding the asset and liabilities side for the three areas will provide a rough idea of overall weighting. This shows that just on 45% of the balance sheet total lies outside the area of influence of normal monetary policy, with around 20% accounted for by marginal monetary policy activities and a full 35% attributable to core monetary policy measures (DM 238.5bn to DM 674.2bn, giving 35.4%).

Table 1. A simplified Bundesbank balance sheet (figures as of 29 February 1996 in DM bn)

	Assets			Liabilities
Core monetary-policy activities	Securities repurchase agreements (SRTs)	131.4	40.6	Bank deposits
			1.6	Liquidity instruments
	Trade bills	62.7		
	Lombard lendings	2.2		
	Securities	0.0		
	Subtotal	196.3	42.2	Subtotal
Marginal monetary-policy activities	Currency reserves and similar	124.1	15.1	Deposits by foreign investors
Activities outside the scope of monetary policy	Other assets	8.0	239.3	Bank notes
	Equalisation claims	8.7	22.4	Share capital, reserves and provisions
			18.1	Other
	Subtotal	16.7	279.8	Subtotal
Balance sheet total		337.1	337.1	

Source: Deutsche Bundesbank, Monthly Reports, Vol. 46, No. 3, 1996, Statistical Part III

Of the five key monetary policy instruments listed above, only the balance of payments component of central bank money creation is a marginal measure, with the four other instruments accounting for the core area of activities. Securities repurchase transactions, securities and - carried under liabilities - the issue of liquidity instruments are open market instruments. Bills and lombard lendings are the balance sheet result of the refinancing instrument. Finally, the volume of credit institution deposits is a result of the minimum reserve requirement.

Even this explanation of instruments of monetary policy using a concrete central bank balance shows that the relevant circumstances dictate the relative importance of the instruments. In this context, the following section will look at the legal restrictions which have already been laid down for the ECB.

2.3 The European Central Bank and the status quo

Although the harmonization of European monetary policy between the Member States of the European Community had been proposed on several occasions, the breakthrough occurred with the signing of the Maastricht Treaty on European Union in December 1991. The articles in the Treaty dealing with Economic and Monetary Union (EMU) and monetary policy are those which most affect the subject under discussion here (see Jochimsen, 1994, pp. 83 ff.; see also Eichengreen, 1993).

In the Maastricht Treaty, the Member States made a binding agreement to establish a monetary union within a specified timetable. This contains three stages, the first of which commenced on 1 July 1990, and which could not therefore be based on the Treaty. In fact, the agreements have their origins in the 1989 "Delors Report", which outlines these three stages, the first of which was approved by the Member States without an explicit treaty. This is understandable to the extent that this stage has no major consequences.

In essence, it involves enhanced, but still non-binding procedures for policy agreement. These include a committee of the presidents (governors) of the national central banks, which deliberates monetary policy, financial market issues and other aspects of the banking sector. A "Monetary Committee" has also been set up, in which representatives of central banks, governments and the European Commission discuss related issues such as exchange rate policy (described in greater detail in Jochimsen, 1994, pp. 88 f.).

In Stage Two, which started on 1 January 1994, the preparations for monetary union are taking on more concrete form, in particular with the establishment of the European Monetary Institute (EMI) in Frankfurt, which above all replaces the committee of central bank presidents. According to Article 2 of the "Protocol on the Statute of the European Monetary Institute", there are three goals during this preparatory stage:

- strengthening the coordination of continuing national monetary policies with the single explicit objective of ensuring price stability,
- making the preparations required for Stage Three (final stage), i.e. the establishment of the ESCB and the creation of a single currency and monetary policy,
- overseeing the development of the ECU.

The subsequent articles of the Protocol describe the tasks and functions of the EMI in greater detail with reference to the Maastricht Treaty (reprinted in Jochimsen, pp. 266 ff.). However, the focus is still only on coordination and preparatory work - the EMI has no powers to decide monetary policy.

In addition to the establishment of the EMI, the first tangible agreements affecting current monetary policy were reached. The core objective is to initiate the drive towards the status of the national central banks as establishments independent of their governments, a process which will only become binding in Stage Three. To achieve this, the central banks are forbidden to extend credit facilities to the public sector, governments are relinquishing their privileged access to financial institutions, and finally existing government debt to the central banks (including long-term debt) must be discharged by a set date (see Deutsche Bundesbank, 1994, pp. 30 f.).

These arrangements, already in force, eliminate the fiscal component of central bank money creation for the ECB, a move with varying significance for the participating European countries. In Germany, lending to the government was only significant during the start-up phase of the "Bank deutscher Länder" (the precursor of the Bundesbank), and that only for technical reasons. Since then, this form of lending has declined to a point where it is now no more than marginal. The long-standing level of debt of the German government to the Bundesbank - carried as "equalization claims" - will be repaid in the period 2024 to 2033. In the case of the Bundesbank, the objective of central bank independence will also be achieved through the withdrawal of Germany's central bank from representation on bank administrative boards.[3]

In the case of Germany, only the obvious abandonment of public sector deposits with the central bank - a consequence of the "neutral" position of the state to the central bank - will have serious implications for monetary policy instruments. This also eliminates the Bundesbank's ability to implement a "deposit policy", i.e. redeploying Federal government deposits to fine-tune the money market. The former importance of this instrument, as documented by the Bundesbank (Deutsche Bundesbank, 1994, pp. 37 ff.), was reflected in the fact that a textbook awards it the same status as the other "major" instruments (see Issing, 1993, pp. VII ff.).

At any rate, the monetary policy instruments will be fundamentally reformed when Stage Three takes effect (agreed for 1 January 1999), because at the very least, they will be harmonized at an international level when responsibility for monetary policy is transferred abruptly from the national central banks to the ESCB, including the ECB. On a certain date, the currencies of the countries participating in monetary union will interlocked at fixed exchange rates only (although they will probably not yet be converted into the new currency of EMU, the Euro). From the German point of view, the ESCB can be conceived at the simplest level as a sort of European Bundesbank. The equivalents of the Land Central Banks (the central banks of the German *Länder*, or regional Bundesbank head offices) are the national central banks, whilst the EMI is upgraded to the European Central Bank (ECB), corresponding to the Bundesbank directorate. To enable these organizations to function properly, it will be necessary during Stage Two to reach some sort of agreement on harmonized instruments for at least several of today's participant countries.

The binding agreements impose few restrictions on aspects related to these instruments, and the familiar canon of monetary policy instruments is explicitly accepted. Exceptions to this include a prohibition on the fiscal components of the creation of central bank money, the deposit policy and the fact that the ECB is not responsible for core balance of payments policy issues (corresponding roughly to the position of the Bundesbank). Of course, this does not mean that all the other instruments need necessarily be included in the ECB's routine monetary policy. Neither is the role of the national central banks in the implementation of monetary policy stipulated clearly, apart from their statutory functions in the Council of the ECB (similar to the Central Bank Council at the Bundesbank). The concept of decentralization means that such

[3] For more detailed information, refer to Deutsche Bundesbank, 1994.

organizational questions are particularly important.

Before analysing these aspects of monetary policy instruments in greater detail in Chapter Three, the potential scope for discussion will first be described and, if possible, narrowed down in the following sections. This starts with a historical overview of the instruments of monetary policy.

2.4 Historical overview of monetary policy instruments

The longitudinal analysis of monetary policy instruments focuses on two specific aspects: very long-term trends in the industrialized nations of the West, and developments in post-war Germany. With the fiscal component not intended to play any role in Europe, the examination of long-term trends will concentrate on the four remaining key instruments.[4]

The oldest instrument is most certainly the creation of money using the balance of payments component, including gold reserves. Although bullion-based currencies existed in earlier centuries, the establishment of the gold standard led to a system where part of the central bank money in circulation was backed by gold. The Bretton Woods system then saw the US dollar supplementing or replacing gold's anchor role. With the end of this monetary system, and consequently of fixed exchange rates between the major monetary blocs, the role of the balance of payments component has generally fallen bank substantially. In recent years, a number of central banks have even moved over to selling some of their gold reserves. Currency reserves in the narrower sense (i.e. not including gold) are no longer expanded by Western countries in proportion to growth in the money stock. However, this is still not the case for many of the newly emerging economies in East Asia, in particular Taiwan and Singapore, which tie up a substantial portion of their current account surpluses by building up currency reserves, thus avoiding the revaluation of their currencies, amongst other things.

In addition to currency reserve management, the purchase of commercial bills, i.e. refinancing policy, is the second old-established instrument of monetary policy. In the 19th century, the "Real bills

[4] Overviews of trends over the past 20 years are contained in e.g. Kneeshaw/Van den Berg, 1989; Kasman, 1992; Chick, 1988, provides a more fundamental analysis.

doctrine" gave this instrument a theoretical basis, which stated that linking money creation to the volume of output - financed by commercial bills - would more or less automatically ensure that monetary policy could be neither inflationary or restrictive (see Issing/Rudolph, 1988, pp. 16 ff.). In practice, however, this supposed relationship is so loose that the theoretically pure form of this concept has proven to be unfeasible during the present century. As a result, the rediscount credit instrument has lost much of its earlier importance and in most countries, it has been marginalized to the extent that it is no longer a regularly used instrument for providing central bank money.

Although the more recent instrument of reserve requirement policy was first introduced through statute law in the USA in 1913 (see Issing, 1993, p. 98), it is already in decline, a situation resulting from the functions of this instrument. Initially, deposit insurance schemes assumed the role of winning public confidence in the solvency of the banks in times of crisis. However, the competitive pressure resulting from reserve-exempt deposits on the Euromarkets made itself increasingly felt in the 1980s, and the central banks thus affected were more or less forced to make deposits less expensive by cutting their reserve requirement ratios.[5] Another factor which probably played a part in this development was the realization that the role of minimum reserve requirements in curbing money stock growth could also be performed by a sufficiently flexible open market policy.

This leads on to the only instrument which has gained in importance over the long term - the numerous variations on open market policy. Although it played a prominent role in 1930s America, open market policy only emerged as a truly international key instrument of monetary policy in the 1970s (see Meulendyke, 1992, on developments in the USA). This was primarily a result of the end of the Bretton Woods system. In the first instance, the great importance attached to currency reserves for money creation no longer applied, leaving room for manoeuvre and a need for new solutions. Secondly, there was pressure to establish a credible pegging mechanism for monetary policy: following the move away from the dollar, most central banks decided to fix their own monetary targets to anchor their policy. Open market policies are well-adapted to this environment, firstly because they allow the central bank an almost ideal tool for managing central bank money creation, and secondly because they make good the growing gap in stagnating currency

[5] See Deutsche Bundesbank, 1990; EU countries are discussed in e.g. Meyer-Horn, 1993, p. 154, and North America in Weiner, 1992.

reserves.

These general trends applying to the Western industrialized nations can be underpinned further by a more detailed analysis of the situation in post-war Germany.[6] This shows that there were four phases, in each of which the money creation process was dominated by one particular instrument. Feldsieper/Terres (1994) and Issing (1994) provide an initial overview:

- In the first phase following the currency reform in 1948, the fiscal component of money creation still predominated. However, this was not due to any particular concept, but primarily to the urgent needs of what was then an impoverished country. With Germany not holding any appreciable currency reserves, its banking system in the process of reconstruction and the Bundesbank owned by the federal government, there was no real alternative to money creation other than lending to the state.
- After only a few years, currency reserves (including gold) reached substantial proportions, clearly dominating Bundesbank balance sheet assets in the 1960s and 1970s. The fiscal component gradually lost its importance.
- This was followed by a third phase dominated by refinancing policy, lasting from around 1979 to 1984.[7] With little change in currency reserves, refinancing policy had become the mainstay of additional central bank money provision in the 1960s, and rediscounting operations now approached the volume of currency reserves, replacing the outflow of currency reserves (in the form of US dollar sales) when the current account was in deficit.
- However, this phase came to an end when a new wave of currency selling, evident limits to the volume of bill operations and a feeling that minimum reserve ratios were low, combined to increase the pressure to develop a new instrument of liquidity supply (see Deutsche Bundesbank, 1983 and 1985). Securities repurchase transactions (SRTs) grew rapidly from the end of 1984, and in 1989, the volume of SRTs outstripped both rediscount credits and currency reserves (*Table 2* shows developments between 1960 and 1995).

---

[6] Müller, 1992, provides a useful description of minimum reserve policy.

[7] The increase in rediscount credit in the years 1990/91 reflects the inclusion of East German banks and their institutional adjustment to Western standards.

Table 2. Selected assets of the Deutsche Bundesbank

End of month	Balance sheet total DM bn	Currency reserves DM bn	Redis-count credits DM bn	SRTs DM bn	Currency reserves in %	Redis-count credits in %	SRTs in %
12. 1960	45.1	33.2	1.6	-	95	5	-
12. 1965	52.9	31.8	6.2	-	84	16	-
12. 1970	84.9	51.3	17.8	-	74	26	-
12. 1975	130.3	86.4	7.5	-	92	8	-
12. 1980	174.3	83.0	46.6	6.2	61	34	5
12. 1985	216.9	86.0	64.9	41.6	45	34	21
12. 1986	220.9	94.0	64.3	33.2	49	34	17
12. 1987	230.5	122.6	57.3	27.6	59	28	13
12. 1988	268.9	97.1	58.4	78.0	42	25	33
12. 1989	308.6	100.0	63.2	108.8	37	23	40
12. 1990	349.6	106.4	85.9	117.4	34	28	38
12. 1991	359.9	97.3	75.0	148.5	30	24	46
12. 1992	368.3	144.0	63.2	124.1	43	19	38
12. 1993	405.6	122.8	58.1	184.5	34	16	50
12. 1994	356.5	116.0	61.6	146.3	36	19	45
12. 1995	354.4	123.3	61.8	145.8	37	19	44

Note: Currency reserves include "other external assets"; acceptance credits until 1990 including private discounts; SRTs (securities repurchase transactions)

Source: Deutsche Bundesbank, Monthly Reports of several years

A shift in the function of this instrument also emerged. In the early years after its introduction in 1979, it was still used for fine-tuning, in particular to supplement the more cumbersome instrument of rediscount credits, for instance when it was necessary to transfer Bundesbank profits to the federal budget without distorting the money market. However, with June 1983 as the last month when securities repurchase transactions averaged zero (see Deutsche Bundesbank, 1985, p. 21), they should now be seen more as an instrument of long-term refinancing. At around the same time as this switch in function, the Bundesbank and the markets had evidently become more at ease in using this instrument, as reflected in the high allotment chances of the bidding banks and the small gap between the allotment rate and the minimum bidding rate (see Beckh, 1986, Table 2).

Moreover, the shift in the way in which the Bundesbank describes the key character of interest rates for securities repurchase transactions - the "repo rate" - emphasizes the change which this instrument has undergone. In 1983, for example, the Bundesbank wrote that "... it does not have an independent key interest rate function ..." (Deutsche Bundesbank, 1983, p. 28).[8] It was more cautious in 1985 (Deutsche Bundesbank, 1985, p. 25): "Changes in bank lending rates ... are still triggered more by changes in the lombard and discount rates". On the subject of key lending rates, the Bundesbank later stated that "... the repo rate is the operative 'key interest rate'" (Deutsche Bundesbank, 1994a, p. 64) to describe the process of money market management, something which - according to the Bundesbank - had remained essentially unchanged since the mid-80s.

Table 3. Minimum reserve requirement for relevant liabilities

End of month	Liabilities subject to reserve requirements in DM bn	Effective minimum reserve requirement in DM bn	Requirement in %
12. 1960	100.5	12.3	12.2
12. 1965	178.8	14.3	8.0
12. 1970	306.9	25.7	8.4
12. 1975	501.7	39.8	7.9
12. 1980	732.9	46.5	6.3
12. 1985	966.1	48.5	5.0
12. 1990	1434.8	68.9	4.8
12. 1991	1516.7	73.6	4.9
12. 1992	1734.7	85.2	4.9
12. 1993	1894.7	59.6	3.1
12. 1994	2007.7	43.6	2.2
12. 1995	2066.6	36.5	1.8

Note: Figures are monthly averages; effective minimum reserve requirement after deduction of cash vault

Source: Deutsche Bundesbank, Monthly Reports of several years

[8] The Bundesbank extracts quoted in this paragraph are own translations from the German edition and the pages refer to the German edition too.

The final instrument is that of minimum reserve (reserve requirement) policy. Two changes have occurred in recent years. Although this instrument was used more actively to manage liquidity until about 1981/82, a trend which can be identified by the correspondingly more frequent changes in reserve requirement ratios, these have now settled down quite markedly. Moreover, the ratios have only moved in one direction - downwards - since the early 1980s, with a result that the minimum reserve requirement on deposits has now dropped to an all-time low (see *Table 3*).

On 1 March 1993 and 1994, for example, the Bundesbank slashed the reserve requirement ratios in two stages. An article coauthored by Bundesbank Directorate member Meister entitled "Minimum reserve requirements streamlined for Europe"[9] describes the Bundesbank's agenda for this process. There are two aspects behind this title, firstly adjustment to the situation elsewhere in Europe thus making the harmonization of monetary policy instruments a simpler task, and secondly a general improvement in competitiveness with the Euromarkets.

This very brief overview of the shift in the relative importance of key monetary policy instruments in the industrialized nations of the West shows a clear picture which is further underscored by the German experience, albeit with its own particular slant:

- There has been no movement in the importance of the balance of payments component for money creation.
- The importance of refinancing policy has been on the wane for some time now, to the extent that at present, it is more a form of reserve provisioning like the German lombard instrument.
- For a number of years, minimum reserve policy has been losing ground to a significant extent. Reserve requirement ratios are no longer a common instrument of monetary policy, and the ratios have been cut heavily.
- As a result, the only instrument whose importance is growing is that of open market policy.

To the extent that the trends underpinning this shift can be regarded as lasting, or that at least no other serious influences are evident (see also *Table 4*), the historical development of monetary policy instruments can provide a very clear prediction of the future discussion in Europe. This would suggest that open market policy could form the backbone, whilst

---

[9] See Meister/Hofmann, 1994. Minimum reserve requirements were cut further slightly on 1 August 1995.

refinancing policy will be marginalized - compared with the German system - and the future of minimum reserve policy will be reconsidered.

Table 4. Shifting importance of monetary policy instruments

Instrument	Trend	Cause of shift	Permanent?
Fiscal component	Falling	Prohibited in the Treaty on EMU	Yes
Currency reserves	Falling	Transition to flexible exchange rates between currency blocs since 1973	At present
Refinancing	Falling	Limits on volume of bills in circulation;	Yes
		Flexibility in restriction (average maturity in Germany is around 70 days)	At present
Minimum reserves	Falling	Deposit protection;	Yes
		Flexible open market policy renders ratio changes superfluous;	Yes
		Falling ratios due to competition from Euromarkets in free flow of capital	At present
Open market policy	Rising	Allows central banks a high degree of flexibility and effectiveness in managing the money markets;	Yes
		Increasing demand driven by growing interest rate volatility and rising capital flows	Trend

2.5 The structure of national role-models

Although there are certain uniform trends in the development of monetary policy instruments, as shown in the previous section, there is still substantial variation between the individual countries of Europe. For this reason, it would be a worthwhile exercise to recall these differences in order to gain a further starting point for the debate on the ECB's instruments. It is simply not feasible at this point to discuss the differences between all of the countries involved, so the analysis will be restricted to three specific aspects. In the first instance, all the major financial centres will be covered. This means - secondly - that not all countries will be weighted equally in the discussion. Finally, a range of countries, at least in the initial phase, will not participate in the single currency because progress in convergence will have been insufficient. Taken together, these factors should produce a more or less relevant sample.

As far as progress in convergence is concerned, none of the 12 EU Member States at the time met all the criteria for EMU at the end of 1993 and only Luxembourg succeeded in meeting the targets in 1994 and 1995.[10] Even if this situation is susceptible to the random factors affecting an analysis at any particular point in time and even after taking account of some flexibility in the criteria formulation, it is still clear that these criteria will be very difficult to meet. This is especially the case for the Southern European countries. At the time stated above, Greece, Italy, Portugal, and Spain met no more than one of the four criteria. This impression is still valid for a longer-term analysis.[11]

The smaller partners in particular are unlikely to dominate the discussion - a rational consequence, because the cost of modifying monetary policy instruments tends to increase with the size of an economy. It is also to be expected, because all the leading financial centres, which could be particularly hard hit by the new monetary policy arrangements and will therefore expect their own governments to act very vigorously, are located in the major countries (with the exception of Luxembourg).[12]

Finally, the instruments in use in the United Kingdom and Germany represent opposite ends of the spectrum. These two "national role-models" are therefore likely to be of particular interest for the discussion, and they will be supplemented by some remarks on the economies and financial centres which are next in size - France and the Netherlands.

1. Common instruments

Before going into the differences, common features - which also apply to many Western industrialized nations in this generalization - should be highlighted (see Kasman, 1992, and European Monetary Institute, 1995). These show that monetary policy is driven primarily by open market

[10] See Deutsche Bundesbank, 1994, p. 27 for the year 1993; European Monetary Institute 1996, pp. 35 ff.

[11] See Menkhoff/Sell, 1992; De Grauwe, 1996, presents a critical viewpoint.

[12] Scholtens, 1992, p. 298, mentions Frankfurt, London, followed by Paris, Amsterdam and Luxembourg.

policy. In most cases, refinancing policy is used as a safety valve to satisfy unexpected, short-term central bank money needs. Although minimum reserve requirements are frequently imposed, their extent varies considerably.

In terms of implementation, the US, Canadian, Japanese, Swiss, British and German central banks analysed by Kasman are all oriented towards very short-term money market rates. Until the 1970s, the interest rates managed by the central bank were imposed by them to a large extent, but nowadays the emphasis is on market rates. In Germany, this change is reflected in the shift in key interest rates from the discount/lombard rates to the repo rate. A problem which has resulted from closer integration with the money market is that market forces are now an important factor in setting interest rates. From the viewpoint of central banks wishing to communicate their position, their task is thus to smooth out the effects of market forces - at least in the short term - to highlight their own influence and thus their monetary policy stance (for a critical discussion see Goodhart, 1996).

2. Monetary policy instruments in the United Kingdom

The United Kingdom is an interesting subject to study because the trends in monetary policy instrument development (see Chapter 2.4) have progressed to a very advanced stage in this country. For example, there is practically no longer any minimum reserve requirement, as the residual 0.35% non-interest-bearing deposit serves exclusively to secure the income and resources of the Bank of England, and is not used for monetary policy purposes. Moreover, at 2 to 3% of central bank assets, refinancing policy no longer has any important role in terms of volume (see Kasman, 1992, p. 16, for 1985, 1988 and 1991). Its prime function is that of a safety valve to cover unexpected central bank money needs. In addition, it allows the Bank of England to provide central bank money at the precise terms it wishes in exceptional cases. Taken overall, monetary policy in the United Kingdom is therefore based on the instrument of open market policy to an unusually high degree.

The broadly-based market for money market paper means that the provision of central bank money essentially functions by the purchase of paper with a maximum maturity of three months, supplemented by transactions based on repurchase agreements. These are dominated by short maturities of up to two weeks. Because there are no central bank money reserves of the banks or average compliance requirements, the continuous maturity of paper generally means that the Bank of England has a daily demand for central bank money.

A more detailed explanation of the techniques of money supply would be beyond the scope of this study (see King, 1994; Bank of England, 1988), but the principle of market orientation mentioned under 1. above, combined with a lack of elasticity in the British system, demands extremely active management of the money market. As a rule, the Bank of England conducts operations several times a day on the market. This form of continuous management can only function if there is a limited number of market partners for the central bank. In the United Kingdom, the system is completely geared to London, and there mostly to the discount houses located in the City. These function as intermediaries between the commercial banks and the central bank.[13]

3. Monetary policy instruments in Germany

It has already been stated that the German system is at the opposite end of the scale to British practice. With its heavy weighting towards refinancing policy and a strong emphasis on minimum reserve requirements, the organization of the instruments is somewhat unusual, although one is almost tempted to say that it has *become* somewhat unusual. This is because at first sight, the German instruments appear similar to the standard international model (if such a thing exists) about perhaps ten years ago.

The reasons in brief: of the six countries surveyed by Kasman (1992, p. 16), four were still using refinancing instruments to such a considerable extent in 1985 that they accounted for more than 5% of central bank assets. By 1991, this group had been slimmed back to Japan and Germany, because Canada and Switzerland had moved towards the Anglo-American line (Bisignano, 1996, p. 23 gives figures for 1994). In terms of minimum reserve policy, the minimum reserve requirement in Germany has recently dropped to an all-time low of under 2%, but this corresponds to the situation around the year 1980 in key comparative countries. At that time, the Swiss and Canadian ratios were higher at 4% and 3.9% respectively, but the USA and Japan at 1.6%, and in particular the United Kingdom at 0.3% were already lower. In 1991, the comparative values in these countries (sequence as above) were 0.7%, 0.4%, 0.6%, 1% and 0.1% (see Kasman, 1992, p. 19; Deutsche Bundesbank, 1995a, p. 31) and the trend shows further downwards (Bisignano,

[13] According to Remsperger, 1994a, p. 28, and Tietmeyer, 1995, p. 141, this runs counter to the objective of subsidiarity and decentralization.

1996, p.16).

It is possible that these figures exaggerate the minimum reserve requirement in Germany due to the coincidentally unfavourable definition of the "Total bank liabilities" reference figure used. The reserve requirement ratios calculated by Kasman for Germany are very close to the values based on the reference figure "Liabilities subject to reserve requirements". The picture may therefore shift slightly depending on the reference figure used, because the Bundesbank (1990, p. 27) arrives at reserve requirement ratios for the USA - with no change in the figures for Germany - around half a percentage point higher than those cited by Kasman (around 2.1% instead of 1.6% in 1980, 1.3% instead of 0.8% in 1985 and 1.6% instead of 1% in 1988). However, such modifications have no effect on the overall impression as statistics of the European Monetary Institute (1995, Table 15) confirm: of Germany's nine EU partners under consideration here, only Austria has a higher share of reserve requirements in % of GDP.[14]

In addition to refinancing policy and minimum reserve requirements, open market policy has emerged as the quantitative and qualitative backbone of monetary policy in Germany. Due to a large extent to the original lack of money market paper, however, it is implemented almost exclusively using securities repurchase agreements rather than direct securities purchases. The traditional maturity of these transactions was geared to one month, but following the turbulence in the EMS in September 1992, this was reduced in most cases to two weeks. It will be extended again "when the opportunity arises" (see Bundesbank Directorate member Hartmann, 1994, pp. 6 f.) so that - including the two- to three-month rediscount credits - the maturities of central bank money creation in Germany are somewhat longer than in the United Kingdom.

Another feature of the German instruments is the need to comply with minimum reserve requirements over a four-week period. This gives the commercial banks a certain degree of flexibility to cover their central bank money requirements, allowing them to even out fluctuations largely by themselves. As a result, the Bundesbank normally only operates on the money market once a week with a regular securities repurchase transaction, supplemented by fine-tuning measures, which on average have occurred just as frequently as the regular repurchase operations (see Deutsche Bundesbank, 1994a).

---

[14] Luxembourg is not considered in this compilation and the Southern European countries - Greece, Italy, Portugal, and Spain - are excluded here because of their sustained and serious problems with the convergence criteria.

These longer intervals probably allow a larger number of credit institutions to participate in the Bundesbank's open market operations. For example, around 420 institutions participated in the tenders in both March and April 1994, with an average of 350 institutions receiving allocations. Because not all institutions will participate all the time, the overall number of institutions involved is likely to be higher.[15] In the case of very short-term fine-tuning measures, on the other hand, the Bundesbank only approaches banks which are active players on the money market. Only 59 banks entered a bid for the 1-day tender on 27 April 1994, of which 20 were successful.[16]

4. Comparison between the United Kingdom and Germany

The differences between the United Kingdom and Germany are summarized in *Table 5*. A distinction is made between instruments, institutional features and the formulation of open market policy. This raises the question of why these systems differ so greatly, and whether one system may be fundamentally better than the other.

The differences in monetary policy instruments could certainly be due to a wide variety of reasons. Harry Wallich (1982, p. 19), for example, has identified three such categories relating to the international monetary system:

- theory,
- the practical experience of the individuals responsible, and
- market forces.

Theoretical differences between the two central banks could possibly be due to the fact that the Bundesbank adheres most persistently to its concept of money stock management, whilst the Bank of England has oriented itself since 1985 to a broader mix of parameters. Since 1993, it has pursued a direct inflation target, namely to restrict annual growth in consumer prices to a specific range (see King, 1993). This would affect the instruments to the extent that the Bundesbank now justifies the need for minimum reserve requirements principally by the stabilization of

[15] On many occasions, a substantially larger number of credit institutions are involved (e.g. Menkhoff 1995a; see in detail section 3.3.4 of this book), which is why - Bundesbank Directorate member at that time - Häusler, 1994, p. 6, mentions "usually between 500 and 1000" participants.

[16] See Deutsche Bundesbank, Monthly Report, Vol. 46, 1994, No. 5, Statistical section VI.3.

money demand, an argument which is lent weight by its money stock targeting, among other things.

Table 5. A comparison between the UK and Germany

Criteria	United Kingdom	Germany
Monetary policy instruments		
- Refinancing policy (proportion of central bank assets)	about 2 - 3 %	about 20 %
- Minimum reserve requirement burden (in % of GDP)	0,1 %	about 1%
- Open market policy	almost exclusively	most important
Institutions		
- Large volume of money market papers	Yes	None
- Banking centres / stock exchanges	London	8 different centres
- Number of banks	about 600 including 100 building societies	almost 3,700
Organization of open market policy		
- Outright / repurchase	outright purchase	repurchase
- Maturity focus	< 2 weeks	2 weeks since 1992, plans for extension
- Typical frequency of intervention	several times a day	once a week
- Market partner	discount houses (8 in 1988, number is increasing)	300 to 700 banks
- Settlement	London	9 Land Central Banks

However, the Bundesbank has always taken account of other environmental factors in its policy, and has not shied away either from defining its money stock targets mostly as a corridor or from departing from this often enough (see Bernanke/Mishkin, 1993; Neumann/von Hagen, 1995). In this respect, any presumption that the Bundesbank has pronounced monetarist leanings substantially different from those of any other central bank is surely questionable. On the contrary, practical experience can explain the Bundesbank's policy, if the consequences of the periods of massive German inflation in the first half of this century can be included in this category. From this perspective, the Bundesbank's known aversion to inflation merely reflects historical experience and thus mirrors German attitudes.

The same experiences may also explain why the Bundesbank still stands behind its refinancing policy. The underlying commercial bills are purely private paper, as 100% financing using government securities - in the form of repurchase agreements - could leave the impression of being too close to the government. The Bundesbank's stated dislike of short-term paper to finance long-term debt should also be seen in this context (illustrated clearly in Gaddum, 1994a, or Issing, 1994a; see also Häusler, 1994, p. 7). It justifies this position with bad experience from past inflationary times, and the result is a lack of government and private money market paper. Another consequence may be due to the fact that the Bundesbank strives to achieve a relatively "long-term" orientation in its money market management, which is, of course, impossible in the strictest sense. However, it is unlikely to be purely a matter of chance that the maturity pattern of the paper upon which central bank money creation is based is somewhat longer than in the United Kingdom, and that above all, Bundesbank operations on the money market are far less frequent.

The upshot is that the institutional structure of a "relatively underdeveloped" money market in Germany (Hasche-Preuße, 1994) can be attributed, at least in part, to lessons learned from "experience". On the other hand, it is still clear that evolved institutional realities, including "market forces", also influence the orientation of the array of monetary policy instruments. The Bundesbank wrote on this subject: "Refinancing operations using bills of exchange correspond to the structural circumstances of the German banking system."[17] This is a reference to the almost 3,700 institutions (not including building societies) which were filing returns with the Bundesbank every month at the end of 1995, of which the majority had a business volume of less than DM 250m (see Deutsche Bundesbank, Monthly Reports, Statistical section IV.22). Most of these small banks use the rediscount credit facilities, but hardly any of them participate in tenders for securities repurchase transactions (see for an empirical substantiation section 3.3.5).

[17] Own translation from Deutsche Bundesbank, Die Deutsche Bundesbank, Geldpolitische Aufgaben und Instrumente, Offprints No. 7, 6.ed., February 1993, p.54. I could not find the respective quote in the succeeding book (Deutsche Bundesbank, 1995).

In the final analysis, neither the diversity of the German financial and banking system nor the decentralized organizational structure of the Bundesbank are the result of any regulatory whim. On the contrary, they reflect this country's traditionally decentralized economic and government structure. Germany does not possess any agglomeration approaching the size of Greater London. This is in line with its federal state structure, rooted in the large number of small, independent states which used to exist in the territory of what is now the Federal Republic.

Of the three factors which influence the development of monetary policy instruments, the theoretical basis is probably the least significant cause of the differences between the United Kingdom and Germany. In contrast, Germany's specific experience with inflation and its evolved decentralized structure, of which the atomized and decentralized financial system is only one of many symptoms, are probably of much greater importance.

It is possible to go one stage further in this interpretation and pinpoint a sort of international specialization in the various orientations of the national institutions and monetary policy instruments. Schmidt (1994) uses the term "characteristic configuration" for financial systems in this context. At any rate, it cannot be denied that the specific structure of London as a financial centre is particularly attractive to large (institutional) investors and market players in general, and that the monetary policy instruments are correspondingly tailored to large partners. From this perspective, it is not only the case that monetary policy is adapted to local conditions, the reverse is also true: the organization of its monetary policy instruments has also become a factor in the strength of London as a financial centre. The instruments used in Germany, in turn, would upset London's specialization, just as British instruments would not fit into the German scenario.

Although this form of analysis views both arrays of instruments as equal in terms of preferences and institutions, this need not necessarily apply to efficiency. A useful approach is to distinguish between the various factors used to measure efficiency:

- A performance-linked concept could link efficiency to goal achievement, for instance an inflation rate.
- A concept primarily geared to the instruments themselves, for example, would be based on the implementation of central bank intentions.
- A concept extending beyond monetary policy which could cover the entire financial system and emphasising its contribution to long-term

growth.

A comparison of monetary policy goals achieved in the United Kingdom and Germany - most readily by comparing inflation rates - shows that Germany, with generally low levels of inflation (average annual rates of 3.4% between 1957 and 1992, compared with 7.2% in the UK, see King, 1993) has a distinct "advantage". However, the question of whether consequences - in the sense intended above - can be drawn from the differences between the United Kingdom and Germany is rather more difficult. Ultimately, monetary stability is not an overall economic objective which must be maximized at any price. Above all, the extent of monetary stability is not a causal consequence of the instruments used, but of the goals which have actually been pursued.[18]

With regard to the quality of the instruments, Kasman (1992) mentions two aspects, the first of which is the quality of the way in which the central bank signals its intentions - this is classified as high in the case of both the United Kingdom and Germany. The second aspect is the fluctuation in the overnight money rate, which should be low; this applies to Germany more markedly than to the United Kingdom in the survey years 1988 to 1991.[19] In other words, even if the German instruments appear to be comparatively "old-fashioned", they are evidently at least as efficient.

As regards the most extensive benchmark of efficiency - the contribution of the financial system to long-term economic growth - the broad range of this objective causes particular problems associated with allocation. In essence, two contrary effects dominate the discussion (see Schmidt, 1994): on the one hand, superior allocative effects could be expected for a capital market-oriented system such as the United Kingdom. On the other hand, a (principal) bank-oriented system such as is to be found in Germany displays company-related information advantages and thus a potentially long-term growth-enhancing orientation, due to the strong links between the banks and enterprises. Although a certain sympathy for the German model has traditionally dominated the literature - due not least to superior German growth - a recent study (see Edwards/ Fischer, 1994) was unable to identify any relevant lead in terms of

[18] Bernanke/Mishkin, 1993, p. 216 talk of the "irrelevance of the operating procedure".

[19] See Kasman, 1992, pp. 22 ff.; King, 1994, refers to an improvement in British performance in 1994; for an extended examination basically reproducing Kasman's result see Goodhart, 1996.

efficiency.[20] As long as the above considerations hold true, this attempt to compare the efficiency of the British and German instruments of monetary policy therefore ends in stalemate.

5. Instruments in France and the Netherlands

The previous analysis will now be complemented by a discussion of the particular features of monetary policy instruments in those two economies next in size which are likely to participate in monetary union (*Table 6* contains an overview). Of the two, France has undergone a tremendous change - above all in the mid-1980s - from formerly very interventionist to "normal", market-oriented instruments.[21] The current organization of French monetary policy instruments can be seen as a sort of half-way house between the British and the German instruments.[22]

The relative similarity to the British system is seen in three characteristics: in the first instance, the French system works with only 26 market makers to implement the predominant open market policy. Secondly, there is no refinancing policy, but rather a form of three-phase open market policy with a basic supply (via the market makers) dominating in terms of volume, a second, more expensive unlimited access channel which can be used directly by all banks, and direct open market sales and purchases as the third option. Lastly, reserve requirement ratios are very low (for example 1% for sight deposits), and the calculation base is narrower than in Germany (currently maturities of one year or less). As a result, reserves held by the French central bank in 1992 - following the most recent drop in rates - amounted to only around 7 billion francs (see Banque de France, 1993, p. 37). Equivalent to around DM 2bn, this should be compared with the German reserves of almost DM 40bn. Even after adjustment for scale, they represent a fraction of the German value.

However, there are also elements not dissimilar to the German system, first and foremost the existence of a non-interest-bearing minimum reserve of relevance to monetary policy, with compliance also only required over a monthly average. In addition, the open market policy is based not only on government money market paper (Treasury bills) as in

[20] The specific problem of universal versus dual banking systems is discussed in Benston, 1994, who stresses the advantages of the German universal banking system.

[21] For a fuller explanation see Quintyn, 1993.

[22] For details see Banque de France, 1992, pp. 17 ff.; Icard, 1994.

Table 6. Core monetary policy instruments in four European countries

Criteria	UK	France	Netherlands	Germany
Minimum reserve policy				
Reserve requirement[1]	c. 0.1 %	< 0.3 %	<0.2 %	c. 1.8 %
Ratio for demand deposits	0.35 %	1 %	variable	2 %
Ratio changes	none	rare	frequent	rare
Remuneration	no	no	yes	no
Open market policy				
Volume ratio[2]	almost 100 %	almost 100 %	Goal c. 33 %	c. 70 %
Securities purchases	almost exclusively	c. 30 %	rare	< 3 %
SRTs	since 1994	mostly	no	almost exclusively
Tender types	Rate tender	Rate tender	Volume tender	mostly rate tender
Liquidity instruments	Treasury Bill Tender	no	since 1994	yes
Eligible papers	Money market paper	Money market paper, loan claims	Collateral	Securities
Refinancing policy				
Volume ratio[2]	c. 3 to 4 %	c. 3 %	goal c. 67 %	c. 30 %
Safety valve function	heavy	only	no	marginal
Quotas	no	no	yes	yes
Papers	= open market policy	= open market policy	Loan claims	Bills, securities (lombard)

Notes: 1. Figure for France estimated on the basis of effective deposits at the central bank compared with Germany, with an assumed relative volume of one third (corresponds to notes and coins in circulation; if based on GNP, it would be around two-thirds, halving the reserve requirement). Figure for the Netherlands estimated on the basis of identical relative reserves such as in Germany, and a disadvantage due to interest rates of - an assumed - ten percentage points below market rates.

2. The volume ratio relates to the aggregate of open market and refinancing policy; for sources refer to the text.

the United Kingdom, but also allows "bills representing loans with an original maturity of less than two years to firms receiving the highest credit rating given by the Bank of France" (Icard, 1994, p. 5). Finally, the open market policy is implemented at a technical level in much the same way as German securities repurchase transactions, i.e. in a (rate) tender procedure with a repurchase agreement and maturities of one to three weeks.

In contrast to the French "intermediate position", the Dutch instruments - with minimum reserve requirements and refinancing facility quotas - appear more similar to German than British practice at first sight. At a more detailed level, however, these instruments display a number of distinctive features, three of which will be outlined below (for details see Wellink, 1994).

The first is that the minimum reserve instrument was split up along function-related lines in 1989. There is a money market management instrument, the "Money market cash reserve", and a sort of reserve requirement on increases in assets, the "Monetary cash reserve arrangement". The first of these by itself enforces a high level of demand for central bank money, a situation which had become necessary, not least due to a desire for larger currency reserves. It is rigidly structured, whilst flexibility for the commercial banks is ensured by the design of the standing facilities. Historically speaking, the second of these minimum reserve instruments is a successor to direct lending limits, and aims to help control any excess liquidity. Its very marginal calculation basis means that it can take hold very effectively when required, and the fact that it is pegged to lending means that it also has a greater effect than reserve requirements on liabilities (see also Ehrlicher, 1973). Since 1990, the reserve requirement ratio has been zero.

A second distinctive feature is the interest-bearing nature of the current minimum reserves, i.e. of the first form described above. Because they are used solely for money market management, which is why the calculation base includes all short-term deposits (plus one quarter of other deposits), a situation where such reserves attracted no interest would represent a distortion of competition. The interest rate is oriented towards a weighted average of market rates, but is generally below the market level and therefore possibly corresponds more to the German discount rate than to the repo rate ("weighted average of the interest rate on advances and the rate on special loans", Wellink, 1994, p. 13). At the same time, this interest rate is the only official rate still remaining, as the rate for open market operations does not approach this status.

Finally, there is also a form of standing facility in the Netherlands, the

"Quota scheme". The quota is based on the average volume of lending, with debt certificates used as security and an interest rate identical to that for minimum reserves. In a similar fashion to Germany, the preferential interest rate means that this popular debt instrument has to be allocated through quotas. The justification given for the subsidized rate of interest is that the interest paid on deposits is too low. Another striking feature of Dutch monetary policy is that it aims to keep the volume of standing facilities and open market operations (similar to German securities repurchase transactions) at the ratio of 2 to 1.

Overall, the conclusion to be drawn from this chapter (2.5) on the organization of national role-models is that neither the British nor the German instruments can be viewed as being generally superior. It is more the case that these have been adapted to meet particular circumstances and should be rated as equally efficient for their particular purposes. In contrast to these two opposites, the French system is largely an interim solution, whilst Dutch practice also displays a number of interesting unusual features.

2.6 Consensus and controversy in Europe

The task stated at the beginning of Chapter 2 was to establish the overall framework within which a decision will be taken on the future monetary policy instruments of the ECB. By concentrating on the five most important instruments (or rather categories of instruments), the fiscal component of money creation can be eliminated as an instrument due to its exclusion by multilateral agreements. Currency reserves will also be relatively unimportant. Diametrically opposed to these inadmissible or marginal instruments, there can be no doubt that open market policy is the core instrument.

The remaining critical areas are therefore above all refinancing and minimum reserve policies. The potential national role-models of the United Kingdom and Germany represent two extremes in this respect. Both of these instruments are insignificant in the United Kingdom, but in Germany they are very important. A (minimum) level of consensus on these two critical instruments between the central banks of Europe which could be reached at present (but based on the restricted sources cited) could run as follows (see also *Figure 1*):

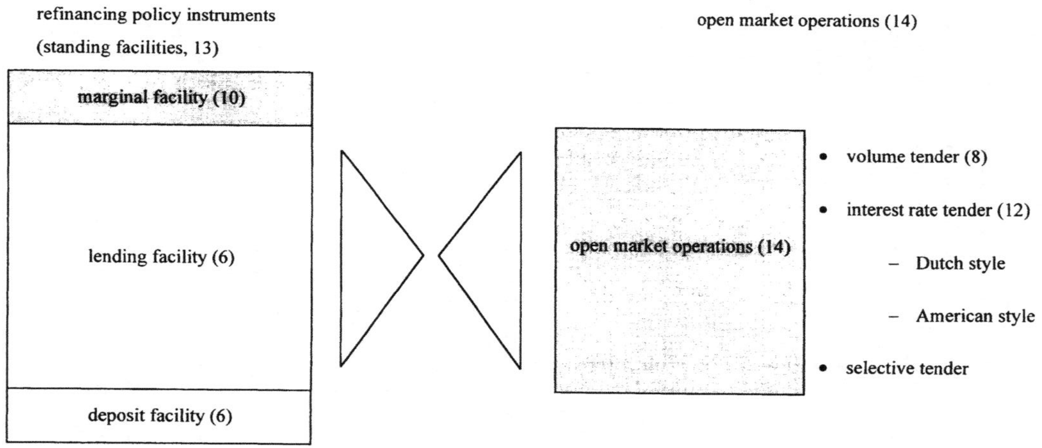

Note: The figures in parentheses indicate the numbers of EU-countries practicing these instruments (EMI 1995)

Fig. 1. Some concensus on refinancing and open market policy instruments presently used in the EU

- Refinancing policy performs at least a safety-valve function to satisfy unexpected central bank money needs.
- Minimum reserve requirements should be kept as low as possible.

However, the need to put these two positions into more specific terms creates a number of difficulties. The safety-valve function can vary widely in scale and take the form of extremely different structures. However, one point of reference for the scale of the function, for example, could be the importance attached to lombard loans in Germany, i.e. around 0.2% of Bundesbank assets (see Kasman, 1992, p. 20). The value for the United Kingdom is about ten times as high, a figure due to the additional functions assumed by refinancing. In Germany, fine-tuning measures or volume tenders for securities repurchase operations perform similar functions.

The only possible consensus on the type of securities underpinning refinancing operations is that everything which has been permitted in the individual countries so far is allowed. However, stiff competition would probably see this apparent diversity reduced to the most cost-effective options. Under the conditions prevailing at present, these would certainly not include the commercial bill.

Putting the second position on minimum reserves into concrete form also highlights the limited scope for consensus, as a reduction in the reserve requirement to a minimum depends exclusively on opinions on what constitutes the lower limit. If some Southern European countries, for example, would continue to insist on their notion of double-digit reserve requirement ratios, any consensus would appear on paper only.[23] If the issue of putting a figure onto the minimum were to be brought into the international discussion, an acceptable guideline could be to align the minimum reserve volume to the working balances of the banks at the central bank.

However, working this out in detail still presents sufficient problems, so that the suggestion of a European reserve ratio "of 1 to 2% of deposits" (Meyer-Horn, 1993a, p. 16), for example, is still too imprecise, as agreement must first be reached on a uniform method of calculating the basis for minimum reserves. In this instance, the consensus is limited essentially to sight deposits, as the definition applied to the maturities of time deposits varies tremendously, with for example four years in Germany, but only two years - and at present effectively only one year - in France and three months in the Netherlands (see Meyer-Horn, 1993,

---

[23] For the rates, see European Monetary Institute, 1995, pp. 130 ff.

p. 157). Depending on the assessment basis, other ratios would result from the orientation of the overall requirement to working balances.

But even an estimate of the effective volume of working balances at the central banks is not the easy task it might appear. This also applies to Germany, where estimates vary around DM 30bn (see Gaddum, 1994a; Jochimsen, 1994a). The substantially lower reserve requirement ratios in France or the Netherlands are even more striking. At these ratios, the working balances which the German commercial banks maintain at the central bank to settle their payments would probably exceed the minimum reserve requirement and thus render the latter ineffective. Conversely, it could be also implied that in Germany, there are either still efficiency reserves in the payment settlement system (see Gaddum and Jochimsen above), or that structural conditions mean that a greater proportion of payments are settled via the central bank than in other European countries.[24]

Once a minimum consensus is described, the areas of controversy can be established. A simplified overview could read as follows (see also *Figure 2*):

- Apart from its safety-valve function, there is dispute about whether refinancing policy has any justification alongside open market policy.
- Any minimum reserve requirement, however low, is likely to be contentious, given that many EU Member States do not use this instrument.

From the viewpoint of a German observer, it should be recalled that Germany and the Bundesbank are directly opposed to the Bank of England in both controversies, at least if one assumes that the Bundesbank is more than interested in "pushing through" its proven instruments, if at all possible.[25] The example of minimum reserves shows clearly that this instrument does not exist in Denmark, Luxembourg and Sweden, that it is not used in Belgium, that it has no monetary policy function in the United Kingdom and that the reserve requirements in France and the Netherlands are considerably lower. Apart from some Southern European countries, which are unlikely to participate in monetary union in the foreseeable future, the German level of minimum reserve requirements is by far the highest, even after the drastic cuts between 1993 and 1995.

[24] Hartmann, 1994, cites c. 30% of intercompany transactions.

[25] See Tietmeyer, 1995, p. 142: "...it is obvious that we will defend a proven set of instruments." A justification on the grounds of credibility is given by Cukierman, 1995.

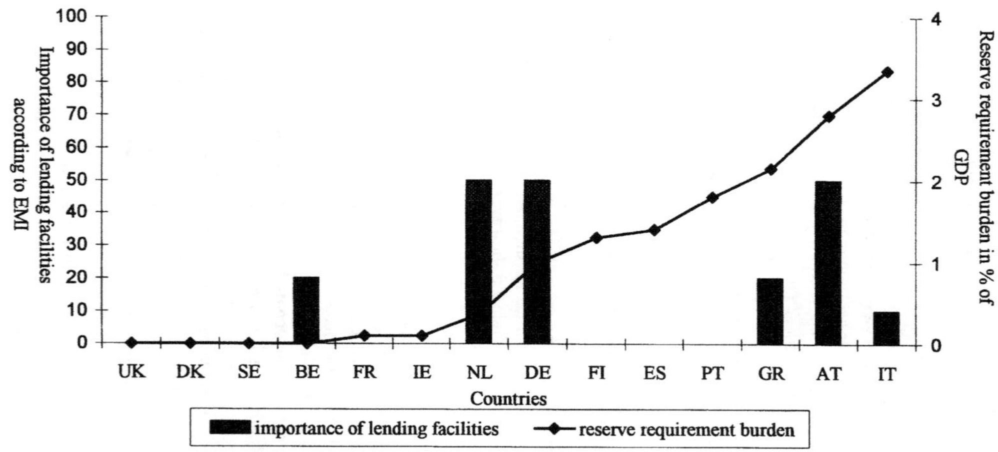

Lending facilities (importance): high 100%; intermediate 50%; low 20%; close to market-rates calculated as 50% "discount" on the importance

Remuneration of minimum reserves: close to market rate: 10% burden; partly: 50% burden; no remuneration: 100% burden

Source: EMI (1995), p. 128f.; reserve requirement for Germany includes the 1995 decrease; see also Menkhoff, 1996a

Fig. 2. EU-controversy on reserve requirement burden and lending facilities

Chapter Three contains a more detailed analysis of the relevant monetary policy instruments and the necessary clarification of these stances.

3 Measuring the instruments against the goals

3.1 An "optimum" environment

Although the instruments will be discussed in this chapter in terms of the goals already described, it would not be advisable to treat them all equally. Chapter 2 highlighted those monetary policy instruments which are likely to be particularly contentious, and attention will therefore be focused in this chapter on refinancing and minimum reserve policy, and also necessarily on open market policy. The analysis will be based on the minimum level of consensus already defined.

It would be most useful to start the analysis with the goal of "efficiency" because this is the basis of all successful monetary policy. In turn, the efficiency of a set of monetary policy tools depends on the relevant environmental conditions. To allow the discussion to be structured more effectively, Chapter 3.1 will assume that the environment is "optimum" in terms of economic theory. This means in particular that there are no relevant information or incentive problems, no externalities or institutional restraints.

This confined, "ideal" environment, and the subsequent gradual relaxation of the restrictive assumptions in Chapter 3.2, can provide a better basis for establishing the rational grounds for particular instruments. The discussion could then move on, not to the instruments themselves, but rather directly to any breach of particular "optimum" conditions. In the best possible case, a set of tools could then be tailor-made to fit the respective environment.

Because the "optimum" case will always be a simple case, the monetary policy tasks should be correspondingly simple: the sole objective is controlled expansion of money supply in the economy. No attention need be paid here as to whether this is a continuous or a more anticyclical process, or whether concern about the stability of the financial system affects specific activities or not. The essential objective is to ensure that the money market can be managed to the greatest possible degree so that it reflects the central bank's intentions.

This can be used to derive the first criterion for an optimum array of tools, namely its "management efficiency". Although this is certainly the prime criterion for achieving monetary policy goals, it should be supplemented by the aspect of cost efficiency. This states that the direct costs incurred for the implementation of monetary policy should be kept as low as possible. As a rule, the literature now assumes that of the three instruments in question, open market policy is undoubtedly the most efficient (e.g. Issing, 1988):

- Management efficiency: open market operations are flexible and can be targeted accurately. There are two advantages to this. Firstly, facilities for their implementation in developed markets are almost unlimited, and secondly, operations can be conducted - with both expansive and restrictive objectives - on a daily basis exactly in line with current requirements.
- Cost efficiency: this is extremely high, because normally large blocks of paper can be traded, there is no need for continuous checks on the quality of the securities involved, the central bank can avail itself of existing infrastructures for money and bond markets, and at a more general level, policy can be reduced to a single instrument.

Open market policy is also a fundamentally suitable instrument in terms of the two other goals of this study:

- Fair competition: in contrast to many other monetary policy tools, this is ensured because there is no need for differentiation at an administrative level. In an ideal situation, there are no quotas, no split ratios, no excessive restrictions on the underlying securities, and so on. Fair competition is also guaranteed by the openness of the process, with the central bank for instance announcing its activities and auctioning central bank money.
- Decentralization: as the example of the Bundesbank shows, open market policy need not necessarily be associated with a heavily centralized system.

In this respect, it should come as no surprise that open market policy is the instrument favoured not least by many theoretical economists, initially above all by those tending towards monetarist views (see Ehrlicher, 1981). In the early 1970s, for example, this was the stance supported by both the German council of economic experts (*Sachverständigenrat*) and by banking practitioners. As a result, the vast majority of articles in the current debate on the array of monetary policy tools of a European Central Bank explicitly advance the view that open market policy should represent the "backbone" instrument of monetary policy (e.g. Issing, 1996, Jarchow, 1995; Koebnick, 1994; König, 1994; Treutler, 1992).

From this perspective, the question arises as to the rationale which could be put forward for "qualifying" this instrument by supplementing it with other instruments. There are, of course, many such grounds which have no place in this study, such as established techniques, or practices which benefit particular market players. The only significant factor in this context, however, is whether there are any indications of "sub-optimal" markets in the real world which could justify departing from the undoubtedly elegant solution of a single instrument with so many advantages. In all such instances, any deviations from "perfect" market conditions must be analysed to establish whether they are sufficient to warrant modification of the array of tools.

By systematizing the approaches proposed in the literature for such relevant market imperfections on the basis of alternative instruments, it is possible to distinguish between arguments for minimum reserve policy and for refinancing policy. However, the organization of the instruments must then be examined in a second stage to establish how they can satisfy the efficiency criteria described above to the greatest possible extent. The justifications will be discussed in greater detail in Chapter 3.2, and then used in Chapters 3.3 and 3.4 to cover the goals of fair competition, decentralization and associated organizational issues.

3.2 Monetary efficiency under constraints

3.2.1 Can a minimum reserve policy be abandoned?

Although the question of what is an efficient monetary policy tool points directly to open market policy as long as no further - or indeed heavily simplified - assumptions are made about the basic environment, the situation looks rather different if more restrictive assumptions are made.

Section 3.2.1 looks at this scenario as applied to minimum reserve policy, while the following three sections examine its impact on refinancing policy.

There are seven major lines of argument which support a minimum reserve policy, as well as other justifications which will be mentioned here to complete the picture. The first of these, of course, is to secure income (by transferring central bank profits to the national budget), a process which is openly supported in the United States, for example, by Congress (see Feinmann, 1993). Others see the minimum reserve requirement as the "price" to be paid for other services provided free of charge by the central bank, although more appropriate pricing of the services would surely be more efficient (see Baltensperger, 1982a, p. 230). Baltensperger also mentions the view advanced by Thomas Mayer that minimum reserves are a "tax" on the utility of liquidity. However, viewing liquidity as "income" means that cash would have to be treated similarly. Taken overall, these are reasons which can be ignored in any analysis of monetary policy, in contrast to those described below.

The minimum reserve requirement was originally an instrument for countering crises of confidence arising from liquidity shortages. By updating this to a certain extent, it can be used secondly to curb excessive risk-taking. Thirdly, a minimum reserve requirement can be justified from the aspect of welfare economics. Fourthly, the advocates of a minimum reserve requirement see it as a very effective instrument for restricting liquidity. The fifth argument is that there is a need to ensure demand for central bank money if innovative technologies eliminate cash as a means of payment. It is also seen (sixth argument) as a means of countering fluctuations in money demand, and finally, there is a technical justification based on the finding that a minimum reserve stabilizes demand for central bank money and thus makes the task of steering the money market much simpler.

These arguments are essentially negative in character. They see minimum reserves not as an instrument of active money market management[1], but rather as one which exercises a sort of safeguard function for monetary policy. However, this cannot come as too much of a surprise; given that markets do not always function smoothly, the concept of a back-up tool for open market policy makes sense. The relevance of these functional problems will be analysed below.

[1] See Loungani/Rush (1995) for real effects of changes in reserve requirements.

1. Countering crises of confidence

In terms of the origins of these justifications, the oldest is a worry that the banking system could be exposed to extreme demand for liquidity - for whatever reason - which could trigger additional demand if it is not satisfied (described briefly in Issing, 1993, p. 98). The cause of the secondary demand is investors' fears that they will lose their deposit money, a situation they wish to avoid by converting their deposits into cash before the worst happens. Because this major run on the banks cannot be met, a temporary liquidity shortage would rapidly grow into a general crisis of confidence. Goodhart (1988, pp. 85 ff.) points out that in recent times, instead of turning deposits into cash, they have been switched to banks regarded as more reliable. However, this only modifies the core problem of a serious threat to the system.

A minimum reserve requirement would tackle this situation by forcing the credit institutions to maintain liquidity holdings at the central bank which could be used to meet this unexpected demand for liquidity. In economic terms, this means that the instrument is attempting to internalize potential externalities. This would be justified if the damage to the economy caused by a possible run would be greater than the inevitable allocation drawbacks resulting from an excessive liquidity reserve, which is what the minimum reserve is from an operating point of view. In contrast, there appears to be no direct economic disadvantage of a minimum reserve because the requirement imposed on the banks is offset by a financial advantage for the central bank, and ultimately for the national budget.

However, the original economic problem of potential runs can also be countered by other methods (see also Richter, 1991). For example, if depositors can be sure of some sort of credible deposit protection, there will be no reason for withdrawing funds if a bank has possible solvency problems. Another factor which can prevent any runs is the existence of a functioning money market which ensures equilibrium between the banks if liquidity is tight. There must also be an effective banking supervision mechanism to prevent solvency problems. Finally, the central bank functions as the lender of last resort to prevent any collapse (see Brimmer, 1989).

All things considered, it can be said that the present situation in the banking sector is such that there is no longer a need for minimum reserve requirements to forestall crises such as those described above. In the USA, for instance, the Federal Reserve Bank has not advanced this argument in favour of minimum reserves since around 1930 (see Feinmann, 1993, p. 574).

2. Countering excessive risk-taking

This discussion, which had actually been settled some time ago, has been revived to a certain extent in the USA in the context of the incentive effects of the economic regulatory framework (and in this case, a reserve requirement). Cothren (1987, as well as Cothren/Waud, 1994) suggests that bank management would probably tend towards an excessively risky business policy in an unregulated environment. He does this by using an argument accepted in finance theory, based on the one hand on the asymmetry of information available to management (better informed) and the owners (less well informed), and on the other, on the unequal distribution of liability in the event of any losses. As part of this concept, minimum reserves could be an instrument for countering an incentive to adopt an excessively risky policy.

Whilst Cothren has developed his arguments in the context of a controversy over free banking theories and draws attention to their potentially negative external effects, Greenbaum/Thakor (1989) reverse this perspective and analyse undesirable stimuli which can emanate from excessive regulation. In an environment characterized by partial deposit insurance, depositors need to be able to identify the risk quality of bank assets, and thus of the security of their own deposits. At the same time, the managers (at least) of the more risk-averse banks have an incentive to demonstrate this policy to their depositors. The authors show that under specific circumstances to be found in the USA, the volume of surplus reserves can play this signal function. In consequence, they suggest, a minimum reserve requirement generally means that the reserves held by at least some banks exceed the level of surplus reserves they would otherwise prefer to hold, and are thus no longer able to transmit a signal to depositors. From this perspective, minimum reserves have a negative externality, because they (partially) devalue the means of identifying banks of different "quality".

Of course the two strains of thought outlined above, inferring or rejecting a minimum reserve requirement on the basis of information problems, only "apply" within the framework of their respective models. As far as the present study is concerned, it should be noted that both the free banking discussion in the USA and the issue of surplus reserves (in combination with the discount window credits unpopular with the banks there) are largely irrelevant in Europe. In addition, there is much to be said for the argument that based on the knowledge available today, minimum reserves do not represent the core tool for ensuring the best possible method of controlling the conditions for influencing bank management (see Richter, 1991, p.60).

3. Countering a neglected welfare effect

A third argument in favour of minimum reserve requirements is based on the increase in overall economic efficiency which their imposition can bring about. This argument has been advanced by Baltensperger (1982a).

The cornerstone of these notions is the argument that government money has a positive externality, in contrast to deposits with (private) banks. This arises "...because of a divergence between private holding cost and social production cost" (see Baltensperger, 1982a, p. 226). In the choice between - at a simplified level - cash and interest-bearing sight (demand) deposits, people will prefer the latter because they correspond to their personal motives, whilst earnings from the production of cash do not benefit them directly, but rather benefit the state. In this respect, the effective cash holding may be best for the individual agent, but not for the economy as a whole.

The link to welfare is seen in the notion that money helps reduce information and transaction costs, in other words that it acts as a production factor. To continue along this line, it may be assumed that cash and sight deposits are not perfect substitutes. There must therefore be a particular optimum combination of the two forms of money which can only be achieved if decision-makers take full responsibility for the costs and benefits. As was stated above, however, this is not the case. If the potential concept of interest payments on cash is rejected, the introduction of a minimum reserve is consequently the second-best solution for improving allocation and thus enhancing welfare.

In principle, there are few objections to the train of thought expressed explicitly in a model. In practice, however, it should be noted that in Germany, for example, sight deposits attract little or no interest, and that the model takes no account of fees and charges, which affect deposits more than they do cash. In this respect, it is not at all clear whether the assumed externality actually exists in such a concrete institutional environment. If one also remembers how difficult it would probably be to match the model parameters with empirical values, it becomes clear that this is a very abstract concept which can hardly reasonably be used to derive any tangible recommendations on how to implement monetary policy.

4. Countering excessive liquidity

In what is almost the counterpart to the liquidity shortages described above (see 1.), there is also a concern that excessive liquidity in the banking system can only be reduced by means of an increased minimum reserve (e.g. Friedman, 1988; Timmermann, 1989; Hesse, 1991). This line of argument apparently lays down two conditions. The first of these is that open market policy is not capable of absorbing liquidity to the extent desired, and secondly that there can be such a thing as a "liquidity surge" in the first place. Both of these conditions revolve around institutional circumstances.

To produce true surges in liquidity, there must be fixed exchange rates, otherwise the central bank will manage the potential sources of central bank money creation too well, and no collapse in demand can realistically be assumed. But even if fixed exchange rates are in place, a central bank can in principle skim off liquidity through corresponding open market operations, as the Bundesbank did during the 1992/93 EMS crises.

The question of whether minimum reserve policy is needed for this purpose therefore depends on the available array of tools. Seen in this light, it can be a useful instrument, for instance at a time when open market policy in Germany had not achieved its current level of importance and had reached its quantitative limits. Hesse (1991, pp. 447 f.) explicitly refers to this case. However, even if German securities repurchase transactions have now reached a volume regarded as sufficient, it must be conceded that there could always be situations in which this tool cannot counter an inflow of liquidity in the desired form. The key questions, however, are firstly whether such extreme situations should be taken as a benchmark, secondly whether other measures may not be more suitable in such cases (for example a currency revaluation) and thirdly whether the cost of the higher reserve ratios which would then be required would justify the benefits (compared with the other measures). Given the circumstances prevailing in Germany today, this must all be somewhat unlikely.

However, it may well apply elsewhere in Europe, such as the Netherlands, where - partly because of a lack of appropriate money market paper - open market policy is not as pronounced as it is in Germany, and the minimum reserve instrument is viewed as a useful supplementary tool. It should, however, be mentioned in this context that the ratio applied in the Netherlands to the relevant reserve requirement on increases in assets has been zero for many years.

Finally, a modification to the above arguments should also be described, one which Hesse views as "by far the most important" (see Hesse, 1991, p. 433). This sees the minimum reserve as a sort of automatic curb on money creation. Two aspects must be considered, the constraint function and the automatic mechanism. The importance of the former is directly dependent on the volume of the minimum reserve in relation to the two other constraints, demand for cash and working balances. In the emerging European scenario with perhaps no more than notional minimum reserves, it is clear that this function will be negligible. The question of whether this in itself will be a problem depends amongst other factors on demand for cash, which will be discussed below (see 5.).

The one remaining question is then whether an automatic mechanism can have some sort of intrinsic value. In terms of monetary policy, this appears dubious if one imagines a sort of automatic stabilizer, since not every increase in money demand is problematic, and vice-versa. In terms of political economy, the silence with which such a braking measure operates may well be welcome, but this would entail firstly a certain dependence of the central bank decision on its institutional environment, and secondly a shaping of this environment's opinion which is inappropriate from the viewpoint of economic theory.

To sum up, minimum reserve policy is not an instrument which is needed to skim off liquidity if the volume and flexibility of open market policy is sufficient. The Belgian, and in part Dutch solutions, where the instrument is available but generally not used, are a sort of lifeline.

5. Countering a lack of demand for central bank money

The fifth reason given to substantiate the instrument of minimum reserve requirements is based not on a disequilibrium where a surplus of central bank money is the problem, but on a shortfall in demand. It is conceivable, for instance, that innovative payment systems - Kath (1993) draws attention in particular to electronic cash - will increasingly divorce transactions in the economy from demand for currency (see also Braasch/Hesse, 1994). Von Weizsäcker (1987) highlights another possibility, which is that the public no longer holds bank deposits with a fixed nominal value, but switches to direct shares in (fund) assets whose value fluctuates with the prices of the assets in the fund. If such shares are then made transferable, the conditions prevailing today mean that the basis of money stock management would be eliminated.[2] However, considering just the divorce of transactions from demand for money,

[2] And perhaps the instability of the banking system as well; see Goodhart, 1988.

monetary policy could easily lose one of its control functions, since commercial bank demand for central bank money ultimately depends on customer demand for cash.

In such a scenario, the minimum reserve would be a guard against the effects of new technologies. "If public-sector cash is displaced by private bank money, the only tool left to the central bank to manage the money stock is the minimum reserve" (Kath, 1993, p. 323). In borderline cases based on the arrangements in place today, demand for central bank money would be established on a purely calculatory basis from the liabilities structure of the commercial banks. In anticipation of possible developments, however, it is possible to extend this process further, since some innovations do not only endanger demand for currency, but replace sight deposits or intensify their use, and thus increase the velocity of circulation. It is also possible to conceive of widespread use of near moneys completely independent of bank deposits, which would even render the existing form of minimum reserve requirements ineffective (see Braasch/Hesse, 1994; Goodhart, 1988). However, the following discussion will be restricted to the most evident problem at present, namely the displacement of currency.

A criticism of this line of argument focuses on two questions: will these forecast innovations actually occur, and will this have such a dramatic impact on demand for central bank money? Nowadays, credit cards and all other forms of cashless payments appear to be moving in this direction, without these innovations having caused a collapse in demand for currency. In this respect, research would have to be undertaken to demonstrate the extent to which a critical structural break in demand for currency could be expected within the foreseeable future, instead of the smoother development curve which monetary policy has been able to deal with in the past.

On the contrary, the question must be asked of whether it might even be more sensible to generally exclude currency holdings from monetary aggregates such as M1 or M3, because it cannot be assumed that the bulk of notes and coins in circulation are actually used for domestic transactions (for more details, see Sprinkle, 1993). An expansion in currency holdings has been repeatedly claimed in Germany too, but this is very difficult to trace. However, if cash were to be eliminated from an intermediate target, the related demand could possibly be ignored in money market management. This would certainly be worth considering if demand for currency is driven primarily by small transaction practices, in other words does not react with any substantial degree of interest elasticity.

However, if demand for currency were actually to shrink significantly or even disappear, would this really reduce demand for central bank money to compliance with minimum reserve requirements? At least as things stand today, demand by the commercial banks for central bank money is based on a further component which - in contrast to currency and minimum reserve demand - is not considered explicitly in the standard derivation of a money creation multiplier: the working balances at the Bundesbank required to settle payments. The volume of these balances is currently below that of the statutory minimum reserves, but if the reserve requirement were to be abolished, the level of transactions known at present would not render it superfluous. This is at least the prevailing consensus, e.g. as stated by the Bundesbank. Bofinger (1996), however, questions this view and imagines a level of working balance close to zero.

The line of argument can be taken a stage further: the sluggish growth in demand for currency is relatively unimportant for operational management, but the working balances are crucial. This means that the critical point for money market management is not so much any potentially significant reduction in growth in demand for currency, but rather in the - theoretically feasible - disappearance of the working balances, if clearing were no longer to be effected through central bank accounts and/or only through balanced accounts.

To sum up, a dramatic slump in demand for central bank money could have a damaging impact on monetary policy, but at present, this does not apply to such an extent to reduced growth in demand for currency, with the currently unendangered working balances used to settle payments representing the critical parameter in the current concept. If volatile developments in payment habits do occur which threaten the effectiveness of monetary policy, a minimum reserve requirement will only help in a few of the conceivable scenarios. Because the central bank would have to employ a situation-driven response, it should not commit itself to specific instruments in advance.

6. Countering uncontrolled fluctuation in demand for money

Whilst the latter two justifications for a minimum reserve requirement are based on a situation where sustained demand for money is either too high or too low, the argument here centres around fluctuations in this demand. The starting point is the notion of a relatively stable real economy, and the assumption that development in the money stock has a causal (temporary) influence on real GNP. In this scenario, the main task of monetary policy is to ensure that the money stock develops steadily, and in particular to prevent any elasticity in money supply causing the money stock to increase too rapidly and thus cause inflation. This was the basis upon which Milton Friedman (1960), amongst others, developed his widely discussed proposal for an (interest-bearing) 100% minimum reserve requirement, which would allow the central bank perfect control over the money supply.

Whilst this view seemed to be understandable at a time when the central banks allowed the development of the money stock to be relatively elastic, it now appears exaggerated, and Friedman is now one of the opponents of all minimum reserve requirements (see Horrigan, 1988, p. 98). In an age of money stock management, the central banks have evidently found other ways to steer money market developments to their satisfaction. Apart from this more pragmatic aspect, however, there has also been theoretical criticism of this argument for a minimum reserve requirement.

For example, Baltensperger (1982) has shown that strict management of the money stock is not the same as the stabilization of development in the real economy. This idea is based on the suggestion that with the aid of a certain degree of elasticity in money supply, some temporary shocks can be overcome more smoothly, i.e. with low fluctuations in the real economy, than in the case of very rigid money supply. His arguments, supported by a model, can be illustrated as follows using the simplified example of the exogenous increase of public deposits with banks, in other words increased deposit demand (see Baltensperger, 1982, pp. 210 ff.). This inflow then increases bank demand for central bank money in direct proportion to the reserve requirement ratio. If the central bank does not wish to expand its money provision, it reacts with a corresponding rise in interest rates. This in turn has the effect of restricting activity in the real economy. Under the assumptions applied to this example, the temporary money demand shock would spread in the real economy at a speed related to the level of the reserve requirement ratio. Because minimum reserves may be advantageous in other cases, Baltensperger deduces that on this basis at least, no decision should be taken on the level of reserve requirement ratios.

Horrigan (1988) goes even further. In a monetarist model with rational expectations, he comes to the conclusion that minimum reserves are completely irrelevant to overall economic stabilization. This is the case if the central bank itself compensates for shocks in money demand by designing its money provision with a corresponding degree of elasticity. In extreme cases, the central bank does not even have to react at all, namely if private individuals have available the same information as the central bank itself.

Even if one cannot share Horrigan's stance because it ignores the probable uncertainty about the causes of changes in an economy, the view held by Baltensperger - to be preferred in this respect - demonstrates that a minimum reserve requirement cannot really be justified by suggesting that it can stabilize and control fluctuations in demand for money.

7. Countering unstable demand for central bank money

The final argument advanced in favour of the minimum reserve instrument centres around the heavy fluctuations in commercial bank working balances with the central bank, and is purely technical in nature (e.g. Deutsche Bundesbank, 1994a and Bofinger, 1996). The core of this argument has already been mentioned in the comparison of the instruments used in the United Kingdom and Germany. If demand for central bank money was influenced solely by the vagaries of payment transactions, a constant money supply would necessarily result in extreme fluctuations in the overnight rate, depending on the level of drawdowns of the commercial banks' working balances on a day-to-day basis.

In this scenario, with minimum reserve levels exceeding the working balances and allowing the banks a certain freedom to take decisions in their own interest, minimum reserves represent a liquidity cushion (see Friedman, 1988, and Rich, 1995) for evening out overnight rate fluctuations. Whilst compliance with minimum reserve requirements over a monthly average gives the banks internal room for manoeuvre, the volume exceeding the working balances provides the central bank with a reliable indicator of short-term demand for central bank money. This therefore involves an institutional precaution to ensure a desired reduction in interest rate volatility. However, it should be noted that this justification, based as it is on the circumstances surrounding a particular institution, cannot be valid across the board. In fact, there are at least two alternatives.

The first of these is practised in the United Kingdom, where supply itself is responsive to demand with extreme variability. Canada is the second alternative; the banking system and payment settlements are very highly concentrated there, and clearing operations effected through the central bank are very transparent to it, and it can then make available the amount thought to be appropriate (Weiner, 1992, compares this with the USA, the United Kingdom and Germany).

It is quite clear that the efficiency of the second alternative is based on the degree of concentration in the financial sector, a situation which does not exist in Germany at present. The British practice too is at least simplified by a higher degree of concentration. In this respect, it is also hardly surprising that the USA, whose fragmented financial sector is more comparable to the German scenario, still clings to its minimum reserve - albeit at a substantially lower level than in Germany.

To sum up, this last justification is also not necessarily applicable, since the central bank could obtain a better estimate of demand for central bank money from notification rules and frequent money market operations, allowing it both to service unexpected demand with corresponding flexibility and to tolerate heavier fluctuations in overnight rates. On the other hand, there is still a distinct relationship between the degree of concentration in the financial sector and elastic minimum reserve requirements.

8. Criticism of the minimum reserve requirement

To conclude this survey, the approach will be reversed by reviewing the arguments for abolishing minimum reserve requirements rather than their justification (e.g. Reither, 1985; Rohde/Simmert, 1986). Hesse (1991, p. 431) distinguishes between an allocation-related and a macropolitical argument. The first involves the burden of the reserve requirement, corresponding to the effect of a tax on deposits which leads to adjustment reactions, which in turn affect allocation. The second argument is geared to the consequences of such adjustment reactions for monetary policy, for instance in the form of the distortion of monetary aggregates which may result from the shift of funds to financial centres with a lower reserve requirement.

It is beyond question that there is any systematically inferable justification for tax-like burdens on deposits, and the fact that the burden can be shifted within the banks - which is why it is often referred to as a tax on bank intermediation of funds - does not alter this situation. In the discussion in Germany, however, this aspect attracts less attention than the specific competitive situation of Germany as a financial centre in comparison to competing neighbouring countries. Hesse (1991, pp. 438 ff.) presents a range of qualifying aspects in this context and also draws attention to the prevalence of the monetary policy arguments.

Taking this a stage further, he discusses reasons (1991, pp. 438 ff.) why the shift in deposits abroad triggered by the high German reserve requirement complicates monetary policy. In this context, it is interesting on the one hand, that the disadvantages are clearly evident, but that on the other, they do no necessarily make the abolition of minimum reserves a foregone conclusion.

Weighing up the arguments, Hesse finds that the allocation-related and macroeconomic disadvantages are more than compensated for by the advantages of minimum reserves, primarily as an instrument for reining in liquidity. Because this line of argument is restricted to international aspects, however, the underlying allocational disadvantage of tax-like burdens on financial intermediation is not taken into account.

The abolition of the reserve requirement instrument is frequently advocated on the basis of its undesirable side-effects.[3] From a monetary policy viewpoint, one argument which strongly favours abolition is the fact that monetary policy functions perfectly well in countries without this instrument. Current examples of this in the EU are the United Kingdom, Belgium, Denmark, Sweden and Luxembourg, as well as Canada, Australia, New Zealand and, to a lesser extent, Switzerland outside the Union (see Weiner, 1992, p. 45).

A compromise in which the reserve requirement is retained as an instrument, but the criticized side-effects are minimized, will lie in the greatest possible reduction in the burden of the reserve requirement. In most countries, a substantial reduction in reserve requirement ratios has already been a major step in this direction. The next step could then be interest-bearing balances at the central bank, as practised in the Netherlands and advocated by Feinman (1933) in the USA and evidently the Federal Reserve itself. In an ideal world, the reserve requirement burden would be reduced to zero. However, such questions are of secondary importance for the efficiency of monetary policy, although they have implications for competition between banks and will therefore be analysed in greater detail in Chapter 3.3.

9. Summary

As far as the question of whether minimum reserve requirements are a necessary instrument for an efficient monetary policy is concerned, the picture is very clear: as things stand today, the unmistakable answer is that they are not. They are not strictly necessary - to mention the strongest arguments in favour - to reduce excessive liquidity, or to counter the disappearance of demand for currency, not even to stabilize demand for central bank money.

---

[3] E.g. by the German council of economic experts (*Sachverständigenrat*), by academics or by banks, see e.g. Carstensen, 1988.

All potential functions of a minimum reserve depend on the relevant institutional situation. A shift in this situation has superseded most of the justifications in the countries analysed here, or - in the case of innovations in payment transfers - the reasons advanced are not yet appropriate. The argument of liquidity restriction could only be relevant to an extremely sceptical stance as regards the balance of payments-related inflow of funds. Thus, in particular the stabilization of demand for central bank money is a convincing argument given some of the conditions reigning today - i.e. in decentralized and fragmented financial systems - but it is still not compelling in terms of efficiency. As a consequence, a minimum reserve requirement, but not a minimum reserve policy of changing reserve requirement ratios, could be a suitable instrument for the ECB.

3.2.2 The advantages of rediscount credits?

In the area of refinancing policy, the discussion will concentrate on the "rediscount credit" as practised, since the generally accepted lombard credit is "only" a sort of safety valve for commercial banks to obtain additional liquidity when required. The discount window in the USA has a similar function to the latter (see Meulendyke, 1992, p. 35). The ability of the central bank to provide individual banks with liquidity in emergencies also falls under this category of a safety-valve function (for more details, see Mishkin, 1994). No matter how this instrument is designed, its importance will always be limited. An instrument that is used in exceptional circumstances and is undisputed by the analysts needs no further explanation here (see also Friedman, 1988, p. 87). What then are the potential advantages of the rediscount credit? What are the market imperfections justifying the use of this additional instrument?

Three arguments will be dealt with elsewhere in this study. Firstly, issues of fair competition (Chapter 3.3), secondly the very fundamental notion that refinancing policy should be primarily responsible for tying monetary policy to the real economy (Section 3.2.3) and thirdly the claim of a stabilizing function of a steady discount rate (Section 3.2.4). Five further key arguments in favour of rediscount credits can also be advanced: it is self-liquidating and thus suitable as a management tool; secondly, it has a desirable direct interest-rate impact on private commercial banks; it provides the economy with appropriate signals via the discount rate; it allows the central bank to obtain important information on the economy; and finally, it is based on private, and not state debt obligations.

1. Self-liquidation

This justification of rediscount credit facilities is based on the fact that because of the necessarily limited maturity of commercial bills, those presented for rediscounting also mature regularly and thus - ceteris paribus - generate an automatic demand for central bank money (see Thomas, 1988, p. 116). It should be obvious that this advantage is very relative and is pertinent to specific situations, for instance in Germany, compared with the permanent creation of central bank money via the balance of payments component.

In the present situation dominated by short-term securities repurchase transactions - or purchases of money market paper abroad - this feature is no longer of benefit to the rediscount credit, but more of a disadvantage. The average maturity of formerly 80, and now 70 days, is too long, and the development of additional commercial bills also takes too long in terms of expansion.

2. Direct impact on interest rates

Because rediscount credits are based on bill financing, there is an unusual degree of transparency for private bank customers, with the banks' refinancing costs, and thus the margin to be negotiated, open to inspection. The consequence is that changes in the discount rate have a direct and - normally - full impact on private bill financing. In a small segment of the corporate financing market, the effect of the rediscount instrument is therefore felt beyond the intermediaries to the "ultimate customers" (similarly Thomas, 1988, p.. 116).

Whilst this effect of the rediscount credit is not disputed, the question arises of whether this feature is desirable or not. It is clear that in market economies, central banks have consciously abandoned such direct intervention in conditions applying to consumers. If this intervention was regarded as desirable, it would be easy to link other forms of credit to central bank requirements or develop other direct management instruments. However, this was consciously rejected in the past, or abandoned in some countries, for example France, during the 1980s (see also Quintyn, 1993).

Irrespective of the apparent benefits of a direct impact on interest rates, it is incompatible with the *Ordnungspolitik* thinking which also characterizes the organization of other institutions and instruments. Seen as such, the apparent advantage emerges as a disadvantage in terms of *Ordnungspolitik*.

3. Signalling effect

The question of whether the discount rate has the desired effect of signalling the further orientation of central bank policy is frequently examined in the literature. The advantage of this effect is most likely that it is unambiguous, and reaches the entire economy at the same time, not just the specialists. In this respect, two questions are involved: firstly whether this effect exists, and secondly whether it is politically desirable.

Analysis of the signalling effects of the discount policy which would arise from conspicuous changes to other interest rates or general decisions as a result of changes in the discount rate has produced mixed evidence. However, this is resolved if the role of discount policy is included. If the latter is unimportant, why should a signal effect be noticeable, and vice-versa (see Lombra/Torto, 1977).

In contrast to the USA, rediscount policy in Germany has still remained very important following the shift to money supply management. However, this is more in terms of quantity (and even here the trend has been on the decline for a number of years) than quantity. Bundesbank statements have already shown that the discount rate is no longer seen as the key interest rate (cf. Chapter 2.4). For this reason, it is hardly surprising that no signal effect can be identified for this instrument (Gischer, 1994; see also Deutsche Bundesbank, 1994).

At the most, it is the general public which can still glean information from reports in the mass media on discount rate changes. This is no more than marginal for the professional markets and, as the Bundesbank writes, "more in the nature of verification" (Deutsche Bundesbank, 1994; own translation). From the aspect of efficiency, this justification is therefore invalid at present, and the public can also be helped in other simple ways.

4. Economic information

The Bundesbank has stated that one of the advantages it sees in the rediscount credit is that it provides "an intensive insight into the financial situation of the corporate sector of the economy" (Thomas, 1988, p. 116). The transmission mechanism for this is the examination of the bill debtors, for instance by analysing their balance sheets.

Some time ago, Szagunn (1970) pointed out that this information is a by-product of the rediscount credit and as such, can hardly serve to justify the instrument in terms of monetary policy. It might be useful to examine the information required by the central bank not already provided (in Germany) by its advisory councils at the Land Central Banks or prepared elsewhere. Random sampling of balance sheet data could offer a simple alternative.

5. Private debtors

The origin of the debtors whose obligations are used by monetary policy is a sensitive subject, as it is certainly not natural for a government institution to reject its owner's bonds or money market paper as collateral. Bundesbank President Tietmeyer (1994, p. 2), who sees the prevalence of private versus government paper as one of the three fundamental conditions for ECB monetary policy instruments, is very clear in this respect. One argument in favour of the rediscount credit could therefore be based on the fact that it is directly related to industrial credit and thus reflects a direct function of the central bank, the supply of liquidity to the economy. This argument is even more forceful if one remembers parliament's intention to protect the central bank "from demands by the state for finance" (Thomas, 1988, p. 113; see also Francke, 1995, p. 151).

The argument is most likely sound, but it does not mean that it can be used as a compelling justification for the rediscount credit. Indeed, an open market policy can also be implemented easily using private paper as long as the relevant conditions are created.

6. Criticism of the rediscount credit

Finally, the perspective on the rediscount credit will be reversed - as was done for minimum reserve requirements - with a review of the arguments against this instrument. The prime argument is that the efficiency of this instrument in terms of flexible quantitive implementation is substantially poorer than is the case with open market policy (e.g. Geiger, 1988, p. 134). It is also a matter of fact that its cost efficiency is lower, although a reduction in statutory requirements could tap some unrealized potential. Thirdly and finally, it appears to be the case today that bill finance is not a "natural" basis of central bank money provision oriented towards the economy, but rather the "artificial product" of the regulatory subsidy for a particular form of credit, although "cross-set-off" with minimum reserve requirements is an argument sometimes put forward (see Issing/Rudolph, 1988). The current volume of bill finance would probably not exist without the support of rediscount policy. From the viewpoint of *Ordnungspolitik*, this fact is an undesirable and avoidable consequence of state intervention.

7. Summary

Overall, the arguments advanced in favour of the rediscount credit are not convincing from the perspective of efficiency (see Szagunn, 1970). Self-liquidation and the signal effect are no longer advantages in today's environment. In terms of *Ordnungspolitik*, the direct impact on interest rates and the subsidy on a particular form of credit are disadvantages.

The arguments most likely to succeed are those concerning the useful economic intelligence for the central bank and the basis of private obligations. However, both of these are basically marginal to monetary efficiency, in part because monetary policy outside Germany is successful without these effects. Furthermore, both arguments need not be linked to the rediscount credit in its current form.

3.2.3 Shielding the real economy

The emergence of a wave of dynamic innovations on the international financial markets in the 1980s saw rising criticism of this trend (prominent examples of this are Van Horne, 1985, and Schlesinger, 1987). The wide variety of fundamental misgivings resulting from the increasing importance of these new products and their stated consequences is very difficult to pin down. This critical stance seems best typified by a fundamental economic reasoning, namely that of the "role of financial sector in servicing" the rest of the economy.[4]

Whilst the debate initially concentrated on the supervisory component of consequences for economic policy, such as the inclusion of such risks in capital adequacy requirements, or to a lesser extent intervention in various forms of price formation, such as the introduction of transaction taxes, Hesse/Braasch (1994) have now turned to examining the potential consequences for the instruments of monetary policy. The goal of their deliberations can be summarized as being that "the real economy should be largely shielded from events in the 'monetary superstructure'" (Hesse/Braasch, 1994). To the authors, the most suitable means to

[4] E.g. Hesse/Braasch, 1994, p. 8; Ehrlicher, 1989, p. 48, talks of "support functions for the real economy".

achieve this appears to be an extended rediscount credit, which would have the result of feeding liquidity to the real economy regardless of events in the financial system.

This chain of thought is based on four elements which will now be discussed successively: firstly the question of the extent to which there is actually disproportionate growth in financial transactions. Building on this, the awareness that this has novel effects on economies. Thirdly, the value judgement that it involves an economically "disruptive" phenomenon justifying a need to respond, and finally an economic policy recommendation that a form of extended rediscount credit (standing facility) should be used to remedy the situation.

1. Growth in financial transactions

Hesse/Braasch (1994) provide a wealth of evidence to show how market segments in the financial sector have grown extremely quickly, in particular at greater speed than nominal GNP as an indicator of growth in the real economy. They point to the growth in private financial assets, especially in Germany, the high level of international capital flows, the rapid climb in public debt and the new derivatives markets. All these observations are well documented and essentially undisputed, and it can be assumed that holdings and flows are developing in harmony.[5]

However, it is probably worth reflecting on some of the causes of this growth. The high rate of growth in private financial assets is linked to increased prosperity and economic growth which has not been interrupted by crises (Ehrlicher/Francke, 1988, analyse functional causes in greater detail). Moreover, there is always another side to the formation of financial assets, i.e. borrowing. A trend towards over-indebtedness would first have to be established, as far as this can be attributed to the economy. Where the public sector is involved - and Hesse/Braasch specifically draw attention to this - the same principle applies: a rise in debt is not an inherent drawback. Furthermore, these trends are not consistent internationally, as shown by a temporary reduction in debt in the United Kingdom, consolidation in Ireland or stabilization in the USA. Finally, at least part of the growth in financial transactions is a result of changes in the overall economic environment, in particular the sweeping liberalization of the financial markets in the more recent past (see Crockett, 1994,

[5] E.g. Ehrlicher/Francke, 1988, and Ehrlicher, 1989, on financial asset growth; Goldstein et al., 1993, on capital flows, and Remolona, 1992, and Deutsche Bundesbank, 1993a, on derivatives.

for more details on derivatives). In principle, free movement of capital and derivative instruments - which have to be "sold" on free markets - most certainly have welfare-enhancing effects (as recalled earlier by Van Horne, 1985).

Against the sceptical assessment of growing financial markets, it is interesting to remember the other side of the discussion, namely the generally accepted beneficial effect of this growth on the overall development of less advanced economies (an overview can be found, for example, in Pagano, 1993). Whereas correlations between economic and financial market development tended to be described more in the past, empirical research on "growth determinants" shows quite clearly that financial market growth produces positive, growth-enhancing effects (see King/Levine, 1993).

Even for rich economies, for example, the ability to deal with isolated risks traditionally associated with products (which is how Crockett, 1994, characterizes derivatives) represents a fundamental advance. This involves the better allocation of risks, in that they can be selectively assumed by the entities willing and able to do so. With allocation improving, one can also expect that the cost of assuming the risk will fall. Moreover, if there is a rise in the number of economic entities sharing the risks, this has the desired effect on prices and volumes. Overall, this means that "risk as a production factor" (Sinn, 1986) can be increased, thus enhancing the opportunities for the real economy concerned.

These remarks do not cast doubt on the initial observation, but are aimed at highlighting the fact that the identified growth in financial transactions can be attributed to a large extent to causes which are in themselves desirable changes to a previous situation.

2. Impact on the economy

The problem is therefore seen less in growth as such, as in its inadvertent impact on the economy. This essentially centres around the suggestion, already made above, that the financial sector becomes "independent" (Ehrlicher, 1989) of the real economy: the former's growth could be associated with a quantum leap which changes the nature of the relationship between the financial sector and the economy as a whole. In other words, this growth may have an undesirable externality.

According to the line of thought taken by Hesse/Braasch, the financial volumes could compete with the real economy to influence financial prices and structures. As examples (see also Hesse, 1994), they mention that

- the reallocation of financial assets requires additional currency holdings, i.e. changes the familiar money demand relationship;
- price increases in asset markets (i.e. financial assets plus real assets) influence price expectations for flow variables such as value added;
- major financial assets are increasingly managed internationally under growing competitive pressure, which results in vast capital flows and thus greater interest and exchange rate fluctuations due to attempts to exploit the slightest opportunity; this in turn cuts the scope for economic policy manoeuvre in individual countries;
- although derivatives also spread risks to non-banks, this effect may be accompanied by lower diversification at the individual entities and basically weakens the impact of monetary policy, which only affects financial intermediaries;
- although some innovations such as floating-rate bonds boost sensitivity to interest rate movements in the real economy, this may turn against the real economy if it is used to stabilize exchange rates.

Reading this list, one may gain the impression that there is no progress without side-effects. When an economy gets richer, it is almost inevitable that assets and the activities associated with them will have a greater impact on the economy. If the barriers between individual economies are reduced, their room for manoeuvre must also be curtailed. If one accepts that risks can be negotiated on a broader basis in the interests of efficient allocation, then players outside the traditional financial sector will inevitably participate. After all, it is not possible for the effectiveness of monetary policy to be both restricted and very strong at one and the same time.

The findings on the first point therefore apply correspondingly to impacts on the economy: these are mostly a form of structural change accompanied by growing wealth and improved opportunities for allocation. "It is the reaction of the market economy to changing conditions in the world" (Thomas, 1990, p. 258). In the past, the changes in the overall environment contributing to these developments were regarded as desirable. Can their consequences then be undesirable? This can surely be the case only if the ideal economic system does not function properly.

3. Disruptive phenomena?

Put in very blunt terms, a fact or a related effect should not be classified as disruptive simply because it is new, it changes existing ways of thinking or it restricts options for implementing economic policy (see also Thomas, 1990; Goodhart, 1995). From an economic point of view, in fact, the way in which the markets are failing would have to be demonstrated before any corrective measures can be derived. For this reason, both Hesse/Braasch and Ehrlicher (1989, p. 49) consequently refer to the financial sector as a "disruptive factor" and continue: "This means that monetary policy must increasingly take action to counter undesirable developments caused by the financial sector, but at the same time, it cannot prevent uncertainty spreading in the real economy" (Hesse/Braasch, 1994, p. 8).

Two fundamental problems are potential sources of such undesirable developments: externalities and information problems.

- The externality can be seen in the fact that some developments increase the systemic risks of the financial markets, in other words they cause possible economic costs which private players do not take account of in their activities.
- Information problems can result from a situation where market players base their activities on information which causes price movements not justified by economic rationale.

As regards the externalities, it is doubtful that more recent developments have increased the risk of collapse of the financial system, for example through chain reactions originating in the failure of individual players (see e.g. Crocket, 1994; Meister, 1994, for more details). Measures to eliminate the causes could include demanding security for the transactions in question, for instance by ensuring capital adequacy, or by integrating market players into the discipline of monetary institutions, for example by restricting risky business categories more to such institutions, or by subjecting corporate departments operating in this way to banking supervision.

As far as information problems are concerned, convincing links to price formation must be demonstrated. Neither high price volatility nor increasing speculation (or increased transactions) or short investment maturities are a poor signal per se of the fundamental quality of such prices. Rather, the problem arises either with situations which complicate the achievement of equilibrium prices on the basis of exclusively rational behaviour (see Guesnerie/Rochet, 1993, on this subject) or with relevant market players who base their decisions on information which must be regarded as fundamentally unjustified (e.g. Menkhoff, 1995). This will always result in a substantial and basically undesirable influence on price formation.

It may be helpful in this debate to distinguish - at least in analytical terms - between three different causes of increasing (transaction) volumes so that the problem can be narrowed down. Firstly, many transactions perform functions which are - more or less traditionally - support functions for the real economy. Secondly, large volumes are a result of purely technical settlement procedures. These can be seen as multipliers of other transactions. The only potential "disruption" in terms of the arguments advanced here is the third category of speculative transactions.

However, speculation in itself is not generally undesirable in economic terms. Many years ago, Friedman (1953) pointed out that speculators force themselves out of the market if they cannot operate profitably. Put in simpler terms, you can only gain if the price you buy at is better than the price you sell at (although modern instruments also allow you to profit from falling prices). Viewed in isolation, these two transactions help limit underlying price movements and thus have a stabilizing effect. This is what allows Friedman to state that speculation can only be lasting if it is both profitable and stabilizing.

The limitations of this viewpoint cannot be described here in detail. However, Friedman's connection is resolved if players operate on the markets to an extent which is relevant for price formation and thus probably also speculate, but do not have a full overview of what they are doing. If one follows the reservations of representatives of supervisory bodies, the existence of such almost irrationally operating players appears to be a real problem.[6] The cause of the problem is that on the one hand, the products being traded are most profitable, which gives a strong incentive to enter the market. On the other hand, the procedures for dealing with these products, including risk management, demand sophisticated know-how which may well be underestimated (see explicit evidence in Glaum, 1994).

Assuming that such non-rational players can act on the market without limitation would underestimate the efficiency of management control. However, a "market failure" will also occur if the identification and withdrawal of non-rational players takes some time. In the intervening period, however, such players could help trigger off price distortion or, for example, their economic collapse could result in the externality described above.

The author has examined information processing on the currency markets in greater detail and reached the conclusion that the price formation process is probably influenced to a substantial extent both by the short horizon of the fundamental information taken into account, and by

[6] These observations are based on Crockett, 1994, and Meister, 1994. See also Issing/Bischofberger, 1996.

non-fundamental factors (Menkhoff, 1995). The introduction of a low transaction tax is advocated as a relatively suitable measure - meaning one which fits the cause and is market-oriented - to limit these undesirable information effects, together with other measures geared more to achieving enhanced transparency and thus the "quality" of speculation (see Menkhoff/Michaelis, 1995).

To sum up, the provisional impression of a debate which is still in process is that there are certainly grounds for viewing some phenomena as "disruptive". However, the misgivings described here are not focused on volumes and products as such, but rather on particular problems in their use. Consequently, it seems plausible to accept that there is a need for regulation.

4. An extended rediscount credit as a possible solution?

Even if one believes that there is a need for action, the considerations portrayed above mean that it is doubtful whether an extended rediscount credit would be the most suitable means. Its suitability can be discussed in two ways: in terms firstly of the intended shielding effect, and secondly of a solution which matches the causes of the problems.

Hesse/Braasch (1994) develop the following ideas: the starting point is standing facilities, i.e. refinancing facilities for commercial banks at the central bank over and above bill rediscounting, but which must still always be based on transactions in the real economy. In a similar fashion to rediscount credits today, these standing facilities are expected to have a strong spillover effect on interest rates for business loans. Because these facilities grow to around the scale of the additional transaction demand caused in the real economy, a sort of shielding effect will occur when the real economy is supplied through these standing facilities, but the financial sector is supplied through flexible open market operations.

To allow this shielding to be effective, two basic requirements must be met. Firstly, it must be possible to split transactions into those motivated by the real economy and those triggered by the financial sector, with all the attendant problems of classification and administrative control (see Baltensperger, 1994; Jarchow, 1995; Remsperger, 1994). If any effect emerges at all, this becomes a problem if the conditions of central bank money provision differ substantially for both uses. An example, in which the "real" rate of interest is below the "financial" rate, may help to illustrate the problem. Due to economic incentives, it can be expected that the relative volume of transactions in the real economy will rise, for instance because such transactions are more heavily financed by credits, whilst equity capital is channelled to financial transactions. Such a shift would make sector-driven demand for money unstable and would also have a - generally undesirable - effect on corporate financing structures.

Secondly, shielding can only be effective if the relatively minor base of central bank money provision can sufficiently influence the conditions for corporate finance. Because administered fixed interest rates are unacceptable, Hesse/Braasch support the key interest rate nature of the corresponding central bank lending rate for standing facilities: in simple terms, the discount rate. This is accompanied by two major problems:

- Firstly, the central bank's leverage is very limited due to the volumes involved. In March 1994, Bundesbank bill refinancing amounted to around DM 47bn, accounting for only around 2.5% of total lendings to domestic companies (including the self-employed) at DM 1,845bn. In view of the magnitudes of the Bundesbank balance sheet (see Table 1 in Chapter 2.2), this minimal base can only be extended to a limited extent. Hesse/Braasch therefore supply no details about the possible expansion of standing facilities, but a doubling would imply roughly the same level as securities repurchase transactions (regarded as useful) in terms of volume. Even on the basis of this DM 94bn, it appears doubtful if the conditions of short-term lendings (at DM 446bn almost five times larger) can be controlled tightly (data from Deutsche Bundesbank, Monthly Reports, Statistical section IV.4).
- Secondly, lendings could have a spillover effect on deposits. The question to be asked here is whether there should be differentiated credit rates, but uniform deposit rates. Under such circumstances, it is conceivable in extreme cases that a wide range of sectoral lending rates could see interest on deposits approaching the lower ranges of lending rates. This could also result in undesirable incentives.

Finally, any noticable shielding of the real economy based solely on differentiated central bank rates is unlikely to be effective. On top of this, the associated side-effects make it undesirable, even if the shielding were to work. If one wished to expand the shielding to a level where it became noticeable, the side-effects would increase accordingly. Taken to its conclusion, this could result in the separation of money circulation, with different conditions applying to real economy and financial sector transactions.

If it seems that an effective shielding function is unlikely, then the causes most certainly cannot be cured (which is in any case implicit in the concept of shielding). It should be remembered that shielding causes all financial transactions to be treated equally, irrespective of the differentiation made above. It therefore affects the provision of "risk" as a production factor or the stabilizing effect of speculation in the same way as irrational players. Before adopting such general policies, measures more appropriate to the causes, such as banking supervision activities or perhaps the reintroduction of transaction taxes, should be examined carefully and implemented if required.

5. Summary

Despite the rapid changes on the financial markets and some effects on the factors determining economic variables, such as money demand or interest rates, it is not really clear whether these developments essentially indicate the disruptive autonomy of the financial sector or - as it appears more probable to the author - a market-driven evolution of the financial sector with disruptive side-effects.

Even if the first alternative is a more accurate analysis, this is a weak reason for justifying an (extended) rediscount: restricted to the volumes encountered today, the shielding of the economy is negligibly low. Any attempts to make such shielding more complete will require more far-reaching measures to separate transactions and financing in the real economy from those in the financial sector.

3.2.4 Stabilizing function of a steady central bank rate?

In a recent paper, Hesse/Braasch (1996) argued that the signalling function of a discount rate which is quite steady compared to the repo rate would be powerful and macroeconomically useful: it is powerful because the changes occur only at longer intervals, and useful because this steadiness helps to stabilize expectations in the economy. The new aspect in their argument is an implicit division between a basic, longer-term signalling of monetary policy - via the discount or another similar rate - and a shorter-term signalling via the conditions of open market operations:

The shorter-term signalling is the traditional one which policy-makers may have in mind. A major component of this nowadays is the observable preference of central banks to smooth money market interest rates. This serves to calm markets and make policy signals more easily observable (see Goodhart, 1996, for a discussion).

The longer-term signalling addressed by Hesse/Braasch is something different. They argue that the environment for monetary policy has changed in such a way that policy-making has become more subordinated to market forces. Their concern is a dependence of monetary policy on short-term oriented market movements. On the contrary, they are searching for an option to signal the policy stance in terms of the real production process. With regard to the real economy - and explicitly not to financial markets - monetary policy should aim to increase the steadiness of expectations. In particular, the authors appear to consider two channels for influencing expectations: Firstly, a steady central bank rate leads to steady financing conditions for enterprises. Secondly, the steady rate helps to formulate, and above all to stabilize, longer-term expectations. These two channels will be discussed in more detail (in Section 3). Before this, however, the increased need for the stabilization of expectation (Section 1) and the possibly more limited power of monetary policy (Section 2) will be addressed.

1. Increasing destabilisation of financial market prices?

When Hesse/Braasch (1994, 1996) discuss monetary policy instruments, they also give a brief overview of the policy environment. In this context, it is presupposed that financial markets prices have become more unstable over time. A more detailed justification for this argument is offered in LCB (1996).[7] Here volatilities are considered from the sixties until 1995:

- In terms of exchange rates, the calculations examine the standard deviation of daily nominal exchange rates smoothed over a period of 21 trading days. The value of the D-Mark versus the currencies of 18 industrial countries varied from the 60s through the 70s and 80s to the period 1991-95 as follows: 0.72, 1.41, 0.95 and 1.03.
- In terms of interest rates, standard deviations on the basis of monthly averages are calculated for Federal bonds, bills and 3-month deposits. As the authors establish that the values involved are quite stable, they are of no further interest here.
- However, calculating the same procedure for Federal bonds but on a daily basis leads to a different picture, according to LCB (1996, p.4). The figures for each year from 1988 until 1995 are as follows: 0.51, 0.53, 0.74, 0.45, 0.38, 0.49, 0.98 and 0.63.

[7] Helmut Hesse is the President and Bernd Braasch the chief economist at this Land Central Bank (LCB).

The conclusion in LCB (1996), which is assumed here to be shared by Hesse/Braasch, is that the volatility of exchange rates has - by and large - increased over time, as has the short-term volatility of bond yields in recent years. Although this conclusion is drawn solely from the figures presented, a question mark hangs over whether this is the only reasonable interpretation. An alternative might argue differently:

In terms of exchange rates, essentially a single major structural break can be observed, i.e. the change from fixed to flexible exchange rates in 1973. Consequently, the 60s are the period with the lowest volatility. This does not demonstrate, however, that the Bretton Woods regime was really advantageous for enterprises, as it was characterized by longer-term misalignments. A further example for this methodological weakness of short-term volatility measurement are the calculations for the Spanish Peseta and the Italian Lira in the early 1990s. These exchange rates appear to be quite volatile, but from an economic point of view, one might come to the conclusion that financial markets corrected politically motivated overvaluations in 1992. Thus, the volatility measurement may not show a trend over three decades but a structural break in the early seventies whose welfare implications are less obvious.

Similar considerations apply to the volatility of bond yields after 1988. Firstly, the observation of a trend is based on only eight values and depends heavily on the inclusion of a single year (1994). Secondly, any judgement as to whether the volatility is high has to consider the macroeconomic situation in the respective period. From this viewpoint, the German unification in 1990 may be regarded as a one-time effect and the years 1994/95 may be regarded as unusually turbulent times for the international bond markets, as Goodhart (1995) argues.

Summing up, the increasing volatility of some financial market prices over time is in itself not a strong argument when it is argued that problems with financial markets are on the increase. Any judgement based on the time series alone depends on the underlying assets and the period under review. In a similar study, the Bundesbank (1996) thus comes to the conclusion of roughly unchanged volatility. More important, it would be useful for any assessment to include the study of appropriate economic fundamentals as argued above. The assumption of increasing destabilisation in financial market prices therefore seems to be questionable.

2. Less powerful monetary policy?

Hesse/Braasch's pessimistic view of the increasing need for stabilisation on financial markets is enforced - as they see it - by the limited power of monetary policy to do so. Instead, considerations and forces intrinsic to financial markets have become stronger over time. To simplify the crucial point, it may seem that in the struggle between market forces and monetary policy, the former is gaining ground. What are the possible reasons for such a shift in power?

- First of all, there is probably a mismatch between globalizing financial markets and nationally segmented monetary policy at present. With increasingly perfect capital mobility, it becomes difficult for national policy makers to influence their own national interest rate levels.
- Secondly, some observers at least presume that the growing volume of financial markets delivers the basis for financial markets to act on news from the markets themselves instead of news from the real economy. One consequence and indicator of this development would be less fundamentally determined prices.
- Thirdly, there may be an interpretation of the conflict between policy and markets which is relatively market-friendly: in this perspective, financial markets make "mechanical" monetary policy impossible as they filter the policy impulses. Only a credible policy stance becomes effective on the markets.

As regards the globalization of financial markets, the fact itself is unequivocal. However, empirical evidence still gives the message that capital mobility is far from being perfect (e.g. Frankel, 1992). Even more surprising, against the background of global financial markets, is the measured power of monetary policy impulses (e.g. Bernanke/Blinder, 1992). Additionally, at least the structure of responses to this policy does not seem to have changed in any significant way over time (Gordon/Leeper, 1994). These few pieces of evidence do not directly answer the question of whether monetary policy has become less powerful, but neither do they add up to a picture of weak monetary policy.

In terms of financial market prices, there is probably no clear evidence that prices have become less fundamentally determined. Rather, analyses of price reactions when fundamental news is revealed show that the markets act in a measurably systematic manner (an overview relating to exchange rates is provided in Menkhoff, 1995). It is precisely this sort of evidence from event studies which motivates Fama's (1991) optimism about basically fundamentally determined financial market prices.

With regard to the filtering effect of financial markets, the point may be not that the filtering itself is new, as bankers and investors have essentially always been forward-looking. Furthermore, despite the appeal of the more recent rational expectation models, there is hardly a convincing argument why financial market professionals should have had any illusions in the past about economic policy or other economically relevant developments in society. What is new, however, are the alternatives now available for acting on (un)welcome news. With segmented financial markets, the choice is quite limited at home, but with liberalized capital accounts there is the additional option of investing abroad. In this sense, one may interpret the increased limited power of central banks as a shift towards a balance of power between monetary policy and financial markets.

It may be useful to remember in this respect that the actual course of monetary policy in industrialized countries has probably not always been in the general public interest. One could at least speculate about whether the low inflation policies of some central banks might have been attractive to the public in countries with higher inflation rates. In this sense, the competition of central banks for credibility can be interpreted as a control mechanism of the public against measures taken by politicians in self-interest.

In summary, one may expect *a priori* that monetary policy is on a losing streak and may have already lost most of its power. Empirical evidence does not prove such an extreme claim, however. Theoretical considerations demonstrate even more that the growing power of financial market forces over monetary policy in determining financial prices does not necessarily lead to welfare losses.

3. Does a steady discount rate stabilize financing conditions for enterprises and expectations?

Whatever the state of stability and stable expectations in the present market economies may be, stability is a goal in itself. In this respect, a comparatively steady discount rate serves the goal of stability. This effect is already quite comprehensible in terms of theory. Thus it is not surprising that answers to a questionnaire from a German Land Central Bank (LCB, 1996) support the general idea: both groups surveyed in the LCB's operating area, banks and enterprises, regard rediscount policy as an instrument for cushioning fluctuations emanating from financial markets because of its steady rates (enterprises by 75%, banks by more than 50%, see LCB, 1996, p. 21f.).

Although the desired effect does exist, what is its importance? On the one hand, the discount rate and changes in this rate make the interest rate margins calculated by banks very transparent. This leads to a close correlation between the central bank rate and the respective market rate in the relevant market segment. On the other hand, the quantitative importance of bills for enterprise financing is very limited (see also Section 3.2.3). This is indirectly shown by a study of Gischer (1994) which establishes the effectiveness of German discount rate changes on market rates. The impact is further reduced by the fact that retained earnings account for a much larger share in investment financing than external finance (see e.g. Gischer, 1996).

The impact of a steady discount rate on the formation of expectations is difficult to measure empirically, but it could possibly be stronger. Again, the questionnaire cited above (LCB, 1996) provides a useful direct indication in this respect. One of the questions was whether bills are regarded as advantageous as they inhibit "planing security because of a comparatively steady discount rate" (p.33). That more than 40% of enterprises agreed with this shows some, but not overwhelming support.[8]

More generally, the question arises of whether market participants would be willing to base something such as longer-term expectations on a lagging indicator (compare Section 3.2.2). Competition for information no longer gives anyone the option of waiting for more reliable, but outdated information. Experience shows rather that a change in expectations can be influenced by the most recent information available, such as the terms for securities repurchase transactions.

Overall, the steadiness of the discount rate helps to stabilize financing conditions of enterprises, but the importance of this effect is probably rather low. In terms of an expectations channel, the impact of a steady discount rate does not seem to be disadvantageous but, again, not really crucial.

4. Summary

The discussion does not reveal indisputable evidence regarding the arguments of Hesse/Braasch. If there is any conclusion, it appears that their line of argument may be overstated. The volatility of financial market prices has possibly increased (but not appreciably), monetary policy may have been more powerful, but is certainly not ineffective, and

[8] The figure of 40% is not so easy to interpret as the questionnaire allowed three alternatives out of five to be checked. On the one hand, the statistically expected response rate is 60%, i.e. higher than the actual figure. On the other hand, all the alternative responses are meaningful, i.e.: a low level of agreement does not indicate a different opinion.

a steady central bank rate, such as a discount rate, can be helpful in stabilizing financing conditions and expectations, but probably only to a marginal extent. Rediscount policy thus has its merits, but they may be not of central importance and its effects could potentially be realized by other means.

3.2.5 Conclusions

In this section, the arguments in favour of the controversial instruments of minimum reserves and rediscount credits were examined solely in terms of their monetary efficiency. The result is most unambiguous: if efficiency is the only criterion, there would be few reasons from departing from open market policy as the sole tool, given the current institutional realities. *Table 7* summarizes the key findings of the analysis.

The justification of minimum reserves is relatively more convincing. Purely for technical reasons, this applies more to the evening-out of money demand in decentralized financial systems, although this in itself is not compelling. By taking a very sceptical attitude towards possible developments, one could also support a minimum reserve requirement to curb excessive liquidity (possibly also to justify sufficient demand for central bank money). In the prevailing circumstances, the reserve requirement ratio would consequently have to be zero. This specific ratio is relevant if the function is split off from the others as a separate instrument, as is the case in the Netherlands.

The author does not believe that there is any convincing justification of the rediscount credit in terms of efficiency, but on the contrary, that there are disadvantages to this instrument compared with open market policy. Although some of the arguments put forward in favour of this instrument are probably sound, they can be taken into account more effectively by other means.

So far, the analysis has centred solely around the goal of efficiency. In the following chapters, this will be extended to include the other goals of fair competition (3.3) and decentralization (3.4). This will result in a reassessment of the suitability of the three instruments.

Table 7. Justification of minimum reserves and rediscount credits

Argument	Justification	[illegible]
Minimum reserves		
Crisis of confidence	-	-
Willingness to take risks	not at present	Heavily geared to situation in the USA
Welfare	-	Does not match the existing situation; very abstract
Liquidity surplus	weak	Very conservative approach: Dutch model
Lack of demand	not at present	Working balances are particularly critical.
Fluctuations in money demand	-	Impossible to decide between competing alternatives
Unstable demand	possibly	Applies primarily to decentralized systems; Alternatives are feasible
Rediscount credit		
Self-liquidation	Disadvantage	-
Impact on interest rates	*Ordnungs-politik* dis-advantage	-
Signalling effect	not at present	-
Economic information	-	Can be obtained in other way
Private debtors	-	Can be split off from rediscount policy
Shielding	weak	Causes of disruption should be remedied
Stabilisation	hardly	Theoretically questionable

Source: Analysis in Sections 3.2.1 to 3.2.4

3.3 Analysis of fair competition

3.3.1 Neutral minimum reserve requirement?

Recalling the introduction, this section dealing with an analysis of competition policy is based on the assumption that fair competition is perceived as a goal. Putting this into operational terms, it means that monetary policy should have no impact on competition between credit institutions. A benchmark for this could be "neutrality" in the widest possible sense with regard to the market values of the institutions.

In his overview of competitive impact, Issing (1988) identified minimum reserve requirements as the instrument which most distorts competition amongst the instruments analysed here (and based on the situation in Germany). Once the Bundesbank had abandoned the non-Bank place privilege in 1977 and the differentiation of ratios by bank deposit volumes in 1993 (a principle which still applies in the USA, for example), this argument is based on two effects.

On the one hand, the "costs" to a bank of the minimum reserve depend on its deposit structure, or more generally on the asset structure of its customers. For example, sight deposits are subject to a higher reserve requirement than other forms of on-balance sheet investments. In contrast, deposits with maturities exceeding four years and investments in securities are exempt from the minimum reserve requirement. This affects competition in that the evolved customer structure prefers products subject to heavier or lower reserve requirements. Although this can be passed on to the customer, the banks still suffer distortion, for instance because some of them have advantages in the securities business, or find it easier to broker reserve-exempt, and thus higher-yielding investments on the Euromarket.

On the other hand, the "costs" vary depending on the difference between the required minimum reserves and the working balances at the central bank needed for payments settlement. Banks which have a beneficial combination of a low minimum reserve requirement and high working balances benefit from de facto preferential treatment.

To avoid this distortion of competition, two measures in particular have been proposed. Abolishing the minimum reserve requirement naturally attacks the root of the problem; for reasons of efficiency, this solution cannot be simply dismissed (see Section 3.2.1). A more gradual approach is to reduce the reserve requirement burden as far as possible. However, if minimum reserves cannot be abandoned, the most obvious solution is to apply money market rates to deposits at the central bank (see also Feinmann, 1993; Jarchow, 1995; Remsperger/Angenendt, 1995). This would offset the reserve requirement burden on the commercial bank deposits in question to a large extent, although not completely. This is firstly because in cases of doubt, the rate of interest should be slightly below market levels, and secondly because these are still compulsory short-term investments - if the banks were free to manage their funds, some would possibly be invested in the longer term at a different rate of interest. Nevertheless, this process could largely eliminate distortion in competition between different forms of investment.

However, this still does not solve the problem of the ratio between necessary working balances and the minimum reserves required specifically for each bank. Even if the ceiling for any compromise in Europe could be that minimum reserves were slightly above the working balances at the central bank required anyway to settle payments, this would not take account of the situation at individual banks. In the best possible case for a bank, both requirements would balance each other out so that the minimum reserve would no longer be a strain. In other cases, the minimum reserve would only be effective if it was greater than the working balances not merely on the average, but also for each individual bank. This tackles the question of a suitable method for calculating the minimum reserve, which minimizes the difference discussed above.

The existing link to deposits points to the earlier function of liquidity restriction. This is also to be seen in the progressive weighting of near-liquid deposits, or in the exclusive concentration on sight deposits (USA) or highly liquid investments (France). However, if the focus is placed on the technical function of stabilization of demand for central bank money, as for example the Bundesbank is now arguing, are the tiered deposit rates still a suitable basis of calculation? Is it not rather the case that an indicator must be established for the working balances so that the burden - which only affects reserves exceeding these balances - is spread as fairly as possible?

For this reason, it may be more appropriate to examine the suitability of a bank's volume of payments, instead of its deposits, as the method of calculating minimum reserves - perhaps in combination with short-term deposits. This would have the advantage that off-balance sheet transactions, such as same-day purchase and sale of shares via a single account, would also be included. This would also relieve the burden on deposits, even if this is more apparent than real due to the need for working balances independently of the deposits; it would also eliminate the incentive to invest in Euromarkets. One argument against using payments as the basis of calculation could be that - as in the case of deposits - there are structural differences between individual banks and between the countries of Europe.

A more far-reaching proposal would combine the elasticity of period-related minimum reserve compliance with a minimum reserve requirement of zero. The commercial banks could be allowed an overdraft (without charge) at the central bank, with a balanced account across the average of the period as the only requirement (see Dresdner Bank's board member Carstensen, 1988). Because payments in the system balance out, this would cut the working balances to around the negligible level of today's surplus reserves.

However, this proposal would not achieve the desired cushioning effect, since the central bank would have to intervene to prevent excessive money market fluctuation no later than the end of the (monthly) compliance period, which in the author's opinion - and contrary to King's views (see King, 1994) - would be approaching British conditions. The sufficient evening-out of demand for central bank money to avoid more frequent central bank operations on the money market can only function if minimum reserve requirements are higher than the working balances. Moreover, the free credit proposed by Carstensen, but not by King would mean - in the same way as interest on working balances - a subsidy for payments transfers, something which must be rejected.

By shifting the focus onto the working balances, the picture also changes as regards interest payments on minimum reserves: why should the central bank pay interest on essential working balances? It is probably not the banks themselves which carry the burden of such non-interest-bearing balances, but rather their customers, as the value-dating practice more or less deprives them of their money for a day. If this is the case, payment of interest would have a highly undesirable effect unless the value-dating practices were amended. But this too would unjustifiably benefit only the customers. On the basis of this analysis, only interest on deposits at the central bank exceeding the working balances could be justified.[9]

To summarize the situation, distortion of competition resulting from minimum reserve requirements can only be avoided - strictly speaking - by eliminating them. In this respect, the most important contribution would be a greatest possible reduction in the reserve requirement. However, if it is intended to preserve the instrument because of a preferred

---

9 Meyer-Horn, 1993a, p. 16, discusses this proposal; Remsperger/Angenendt, 1995, take issue.

passive stance on the money market, the following points should be considered:

- In theory, minimum reserves apply to payments in the justification described here, so that thought should be given as to whether the calculation method should be linked to payment transactions rather than deposits.
- However, this concept requires empirical review in the European context to establish the consequences of implementation and the organization to be preferred. Possible criteria include linking the basis of calculation to the working balances, the stability of this link across different banks and countries, and its stability in the face of evasive reactions.
- Payment of interest on the working balances must be ruled out as long as the burden is already carried by bank customers.
- Because the cushioning function will only take effect if minimum reserves clearly exceed the working balances, the estimated difference should attract interest at a rate only just below the money market rate, which could be most simply spread across the total volume.
- A number of secondary questions must also be answered: the number of banks to which reserve requirements should apply (see Borchert, 1986), whether vault cash should be deducted (which happens in full in the USA but has recently been dropped in Germany) and organizational details, such as the time-lag between establishment of the basis of calculation and compliance (see von Hagen, 1987).

3.3.2 Equitable rediscount quotas?

Although Issing believes that the distortion of competition caused by minimum reserves is more problematic than that of discount policy, the disputes surrounding the latter have been heftier. To be able to understand the arguments, it is necessary to review the principles of the quota system (see Deutsche Bundesbank, 1975). The distribution of the rediscount quotas amongst the banks, limiting the total amount of particularly advantageous central bank credit available at the discount rate, is calculated according to three criteria (presented here in simplified form):[10]

- The relationship to the bank's capital is less than proportionate.

[10] See Issing/Rudolph, 1988, on incidental aspects of this calculation.

- It is proportionate to the share of business volume accounted for by short- and medium-term lendings to customers.
- It is based on past quota utilization, with non-utilization subject to a discretionary cut in the quota.

The consequence is that relatively small banks with strong capital and a relatively large proportion of short-term customer lendings, and which are in a position to mobilize sufficient levels of bill operations, have particularly good access to this "cheap" source of credit. In the past, the public sector banks in particular believed that they were disadvantaged by these distribution principles (e.g. Geiger, 1988, p. 135); how is this then justified by the Bundesbank (e.g. Thomas, 1988, p. 118)?

In the first instance, the Bundesbank is not interested in servicing the banks to the same extent, whatever this may be, but in implementing distribution in accordance with criteria based on monetary policy. The rediscount credit therefore represents a short-term instrument of central bank money provision, linked to the corresponding transactions - in this case discount credits - of the banks (structural component). Moreover, central bank credit is directed towards those banks with an excellent quality standing (capital component). Finally, unutilized quotas represent an undesirable freedom for the banks, at least as far as the current array of monetary policy tools is concerned, and are therefore trimmed (discretionary component).

In a fundamental study assessing the various arguments, Issing/Rudolph (1988) came to the conclusion that the structural component in particular causes a number of problems, because short-term business is only allowed in proportion to total business. This may have the most peculiar effect of a reduction in the quota resulting merely from an expansion in long-term lendings. It also discriminates against competitors with a stronger long-term lending structure. The remedy proposed by the authors is to allow short-term and medium-term business without qualification. The calculation of the quotas could also be put on a broader basis, for instance as in the Netherlands, where total lendings are used to calculate the quotas.

The capital component has also been attacked from time to time, above all because some banks did not have the same ability as others to increase it.[11] The alternative proposed was the balance sheet total. This is rejected by Issing/Rudolph because it is a "relatively heavily fluctuating variable"

[11] See the reference to relevant remarks by savings banks President Geiger in Issing/Rudolph, 1988, p.68.

(Issing/Rudolph, 1988, p.68). However, if Bundesbank intentions are taken as the sole benchmark, a certain degree of fluctuation in the variable, as long as it is embedded in a clear trend and can be evened out, is probably not a decisive criterion. A perfectly legitimate question, on the other hand, is why credit standing is measured by absolute capital, as this implies that large banks are better than small ones. In this respect, one would rather expect that the variable would be qualified by a qualitiy standing component.

Although these discussions about equitable distribution are always based on current Bundesbank practice and are thus automatically geared towards a pragmatic approach, the question arises of whether there could also be a theoretical form of quota establishment. If it can be accepted that the rediscount credit no longer serves to provide the economy directly with short-term credit, but is merely a component of central bank money provision not linked to any particular utilization by the banks, an analysis from the viewpoint of competition policy will focus on the subsidy component of this instrument. The resulting task is to "distribute" this subsidy - which should be kept as low as possible - equitably among the banks. This demands firstly that there should be no link whatsoever to any particular business activity (such as any type of lendings), and secondly that the calculation of rediscount quotas must be divorced from the calculation of minimum reserves. It appears preferable to gear both sides of the central bank balance sheet independently to ensure fair competition.

The one element which would be an "equitable" basis for banks with different core activities is one which is generally scarce when banking services are produced: equity capital. A preliminary calculation (see *Table 8*) shows that the result of its effect on the bank categories is very close to the concept advanced by Issing/Rudolph (1988).

As it is currently calculated by the Bundesbank, the capital component has one unusual feature which has been practically ignored in the debate: this is the progressive weighting which discriminates against large banks. The justification given for this is that it helps prevent concentration. In the author's opinion, there can be no doubt that these are irrelevant considerations, and that this arrangement is untenable under the goal of fair competition being analysed here. It is possible that the Bundesbank will also modify its position in this respect, as it has eliminated all differences based on the size of banks - the non-Bank place privilege and progressive differentiation - in the calculation of minimum reserve requirements.

Table 8. Exemplary allocation of rediscount quotas

Institutions	Bundesbank in DM bn	Issing/Rudolph in DM bn	Equity capital in DM bn
Commercial banks	27 444	22 935	21 307
(Money center banks)	(10 407)	(10 336)	(9 595)
Landesbanken	2 846	6 123	6 821
Savings banks	13 399	13 962	14 593
Cooperative apex banks	1 564	2 406	2 841
Cooperative banks	11 140	9 901	8 825
Others	3 051	4 118	5 057
Total	59 444	59 445	59 444

Note: The data are based on Issing/Rudolph (1988) and refer to the end of 1986. The allocation of rediscount credits was estimated by Issing/Rudolph (p. 79; for their proposal p. 97; allocation according to equity capital p. 97)

Although the current method used by the Bundesbank to calculate rediscount credit quotas is accepted by the German banking industry despite all the criticism, the transition to a European monetary policy will automatically result in a review, either because many countries simply do not have this sort of quota, or because it is calculated differently, as in the Netherlands. Alternative calculation methods mentioned range from the balance sheet total, through total lendings, a combination of short-term lendings plus equity capital or a proportion of short-term lendings plus equity capital, to equity capital alone.

To summarize the analysis in terms of competition policy, one can only concur with Issing (1988a), who leaves little room for doubt in his underlying position that the only solution for quotas which does not distort competition is their elimination (see also Issing/Rudolph, 1988). However, if this instrument must be preserved for other reasons, a number of lessons can be drawn from the discussion of rediscount quotas:

- The assets eligible for presentation should not be restricted to bills alone. The more that is allowed, the less distortion of competition there will be.
- If the original Bundesbank criteria are retained for calculating the quotas, suggestions for modifying both the structural and the capital component have been discussed above.

- It also appears worth considering eliminating any link to specific business activities in the method of calculating a quota arrangement.
- As in the case of minimum reserve requirements, distortion can be reduced by the payment of more market-oriented interest, if the instrument itself is not to be abandoned (both Issing/Rudolph, 1988, pp. 102 ff. and Menkhoff, 1995a, discuss this in greater detail). The discount rate could be more flexibly structured, for instance by linking it to the repo rate.

3.3.3 Securities repurchase transactions: an *Ordnungspolitik* analysis

Of the three instruments analysed here, open market operations in general, and of the German instruments securities repurchase transactions (SRTs) in particular, are regarded as having the least impact on competition. But misgivings about this tool, mostly in the context of possible discrimination against smaller banks, have also been expressed in the literature (Beck, 1986, and Issing, 1988, summarize this issue).

The arguments are that small banks cannot participate to the same extent in repurchase transactions because they have serious problems of disposal on the market if they are caught unawares by a large allocation (see e.g. Krupp, 1996, p. 9). The cause of this lies in the infrequent money market dealings by smaller banks, for whom the lack of volume means that this business is not worthwhile. They do not have dealing limits with other banks and as otherwise unknown market players, have problems being active on an occasional basis. There is thus a size-related difference. How relevant is this problem to distortion of competition?

Two qualifications should be remembered in this context. In the first instance, unexpectedly large allocations only arise - in principle - with volume tenders if bid allocation is proportionately reduced to an extent initially unknown to the banks and a bank has bid for a large volume for fear of otherwise receiving too little. However, the majority of all SRTs are now in the form of interest tenders, where this critical effect does not apply to the same extent, as allocation depends solely on the interest rate-volume combination demanded by each bank. Nevertheless, over the last years, the repartiation issue has become relevant for interest rate tenders as well, as the standard deviation of banks' bids has decreased and the marginal interest rate attracted high proportions of the total bids. Secondly, there is only discrimination against smaller banks if volumes are passed from large to small market players at "exaggerated" prices. The key factor here is whether competition functions; if so, then this effect should not occur.

Whilst these arguments are ultimately based on a lack of competition, something about which the banks affected evidently do not complain, there are stronger arguments associated with *Ordnungspolitik.* These state that monetary policy instruments should not allow any "upper-class" and "lower-class" commercial banks, which Remsperger[12] sees as the case if "a handful of banks operate with a direct money market line to the central bank, but many banks have to live without it". Land Central Bank President Jochimsen (1993, p. 5) also comes out in favour of allowing the largest possible number of banks "direct access to central bank credit".[13] The advantages of the smaller group may lie in superior information, a consequently enhanced image, and in borderline cases access to a scarce commodity, namely central bank money (similarly in Holland, 1970, pp. 139 f.).

With the trend towards increased money market operations by the central banks, this fundamental argument from the viewpoint of *Ordnungspolitik* has also gained practical relevance. "For technical reasons alone, however, regular fine-tuning measures cannot be implemented in concert with all European credit institutions" (Schulmann, 1994) and thus lead necessarily to preferential treatment, in particular of large market operators at major financial centres.

Even if there were no directly quantifiable economic discrimination against smaller banks in the context of regular repurchase transactions, this does not apply to fine-tuning measures; furthermore, there may be indirect disadvantages of the type mentioned above, and potential handicaps in the future or in critical market situations. In this respect, it is hardly surprising that in a recent survey by the German Savings Bank and Giro Association *(Deutscher Sparkassen- und Giroverband)*, a substantial number of members believed that the general provision of central bank money by means of repurchase operations was not to their advantage.

Concrete factors contributing to discrimination include:

- At its most flagrant, the exclusive contact between the central bank and a small number of market makers.
- The direct contact with a handful of banks normally required to be

---

[12] Remsperger, 1994, p. 265; see also Tietmeyer, 1995, p. 142; Jerger/Menkhoff, 1995.

[13] This argument is also supported by Land Central Bank President Krupp (1996).

able to implement fine-tuning measures quickly (see Geiger, 1982, p. 204).
- Lower limits in repurchase transaction tenders; these may make sense for technical reasons, but effectively exclude some banks as market operators (the limit in Germany is currently DM 1m).

To counter these problems, technical innovations could be used in future, for example to offer and allocate open market operations in some form of electronic exchange. This would tend to increase the speed of settlement irrespective of the number of participants. Using such a system, central bank money could also be offered across Europe in a standard tendering procedure. For this reason alone, steps can be taken in this direction. The question remains, however, of whether this solution will eliminate the critical differences in information. If this could be solved easily, there would be no more trading floor systems, neither above all would there be any financial centres concentrated in particular locations. Consequently, technical innovations of this type could probably help enhance the competitive position of small banks in repurchase transactions, but they would not prevent large market operators - and in particular those located in major financial centres - gaining information advantages.

Because *Ordnungspolitik* considerations would wish to prevent even the potential existence of a "class society", even in a situation where competition is generally functioning, it is surprising that one of the lobbyists involved believes that securities repurchase transactions have "no impact on competition".[14] Firstly, however, not all of the institutions he represents are small market operators, such as the *Landesbanken* and the large savings banks.[15] Secondly, attitudes against rediscount quotas, regarded as unfair, may have influenced the judgement at the time, and third and finally, the extent and nature of open market policy has changed dramatically since 1987/88. As use of this instrument has grown, sensitivity to any discrimination has risen accordingly, and the increasing importance of fine-tuning measures has indeed focused attention on the "class society" of the banks.

[14] According to former President Geiger of the German Savings Bank and Giro Association; see Geiger, 1988, p. 142.

[15] The balance sheet volume of most *Landesbanken* puts them amongst the top thirty banks in Germany (out of almost 3,700).

3.3.4 Securities repurchase transactions: participation data analysis

It is in the nature of an *Ordnungspolitik* analysis to argue in qualitative terms. For this reason, it may be interesting to establish whether the arguments provided can be substantiated in an empirical approach. The starting point in this section is therefore the same as in the last one, i.e. the complaint of some smaller banks that they are disadvantaged over larger banks in the use of securities repurchase transactions (SRTs). The theoretical considerations backing the empirical work are as follows:

If the money market is perfect and transaction costs do not matter, then no difference should be expected regarding the information-related and institutional circumstances of various forms of discount policy and SRTs. An implication of this view would be that the participation of banks in these various forms does not differ systematically with respect to such circumstances. To put it the other way round: if participation depends on the characteristics of instruments which affect banks depending on their size, then these instruments are not neutral towards banks and thus influence the structure of competition. There are two potentially relevant circumstances:

- The degree of insecurity in allocating central bank money which requires a more or less active money market dealing desk. Because of this institutional requirement, it could be supposed that smaller banks have a higher preference for instruments which inhibit low risk in *allocating amounts* of money.
- The second argument relates to the *price* of central bank money. Banks which are less involved in money market business, i.e. have less information, might have a higher preference for instruments which do not leave them in a risky position about bidding. Their risk would be to make bids which are not competitive.

Transferring these considerations to the concrete instruments, it is obvious that the discount policy, offering fixed amounts and prices, should be the instrument favoured by smaller banks over SRTs. This and related hypotheses can be tested only under two major restrictions:

- Firstly, there are no statistics available on participation by banks in monetary policy instruments and the size of these respective banks. However, interviews with market participants make it clear that at least an approximate relationship between size and participation can be expected. There is a reasonable basis for assuming that an increasing number of participating banks is due to an increasing share accounted for by smaller banks.

- Secondly, it must be assumed that all other circumstances are the same, except the kind of policy instrument under review. This is, of course, a simplification which will be discussed in greater detail later.

Coming to the German case, no formal test is necessary to recognize that the discount policy is indeed the instrument of choice of the banks. Whereas most of Germany's close on 3,700 banks use this instrument for receiving central bank money, the maximum number of banks bidding at an open market auction was 1,485 for the volume tender on 2 May 1991. At close on 1,500, however, this number is a vast exaggeration of the more usual case, which is characterized in recent years by the participation of about 300 - 700 banks.

Although this comparison of participation data runs counter to the expectation that institutional circumstances are irrelevant, it does not prove much. The reason is that discount policy and SRTs differ in several respects, each of which might be important for decisions on participation. Firstly, rediscount credit is characterized by a much longer maturity and, secondly, by a more advantageous price. Although maturity may be not such an important argument - as longer-term SRTs typically receive even less participation than shorter ones - the suspected element of subsidy cannot be ignored. Generally, there is consensus that the complete allocation of rediscount quotas requires a price subsidy, but that an allocation via auctions occurs at or close to market prices.

The following examination about risk and participation is therefore restricted to SRTs (the data base is the same as in Menkhoff (1996a), the procedure is very similar). To avoid any influence by the auction type, the data period starts in August 1988, i.e. it considers only American-style auctions and no Dutch-style auctions. As the maturity appears to influence participation in SRTs, the autumn of 1992, when the common maturity changed from four weeks to two weeks, marks a structural break. Finally, a key question regarding participation is whether there is any difference in volume versus interest rate tenders. To sum up, this leads to four different cases: volume and interest rate tenders in two subperiods between August 1988 and January 1996.

As the next step in an attempt at avoiding structural influences on the comparison of tender types, the total number of auctions was filtered to establish the standard cases and to ignore cases with specific characteristics. The result is shown in *Table 9*.

Table 9. Participation at German securities repurchase transactions

Data period	Kind of events	Number of events [n]	Average number of participating banks [n]	Median number of participating banks [n]	Average proportion of successfully bidding banks [%]	Average sum of liquidity demanded [DM bn.]	Average ratio of liquidity supplied and demanded [%]
8.1988-	Total	480	633.2	593.5		80.2	44.60
1.1996	volume tender	129	814.3	758.0	100.00	140.6	35.51
	interest rate tender	351	568.3	544.0	48.07	58.0	48.07
8.1988-	Total	292	667.2	626.5		105.7	45.45
1.1996	volume tender	101	747.3	694.0	100.00	153.9	38.48
Standard*	interest rate tender	191	624.8	589.0	77.39	80.1	49.13
8.1988-	Total	124	868.7	824.0		60.3	33.13
9.1992	volume tender	29	1139.5	1265.0	100.00	87.3	20.69
Standard*	interest rate tender	95	786.0	790.0	69.32	52.1	43.47
	*v.t./i.t.-Wilcoxon w***			*5.53*			
10.1992-	Total	168	518.4	477.5		139.1	54.54
1.1996	volume tender	72	589.4	604.0	100.00	180.8	45.65
Standard*	interest rate tender	96	465.2	451.0	85.37	107.9	61.21
	*v.t./i.t.-Wilcoxon w***			*5.24*			

* Standard auctions are those of 27-29 days maturity until 9.1992 and 13-15 days maturity thereafter.
** Significance at 1%-level needs w>2,3263.

A non-parametric test confirms the rough impression from the figures: there is a significant difference in the lower participation in interest rate tenders compared with the higher participation in volume tenders. On the basis of the considerations above, this may be interpreted as evidence of the importance of the higher risk of interest rate tenders for smaller participating banks.

Similar to the discussion about rediscount credit versus SRTs, the question arises, however, of whether the difference in participation according to tender type may be influenced by a respective price advantage of volume tenders against interest rate tenders. To examine this effect, it is necessary to establish appropriate market rates. This is quite easy for the first subperiod, when the four-week tenders are roughly matched by monthly money, but not the case for the second subperiod, when the maturity was only about 14 days. Because no such 14-day rate is published, it is often assumed that the overnight interest rate is the appropriate market rate to be taken. Interviews with practitioners revealed, however, that there is in fact a kind of market for 14-day money, at least around tender auctions, and that the relevant interest rate is not necessarily the same as the overnight interest rate.

It therefore appears reasonable to construct a 14-day money-market rate by using the information from daily, one-month and three-month rates. To employ as few restrictions as possible, the shape of the yield curve is not determined in advance. On the contrary, three equations are used simultaneously, each assuming either a normal, a flat or an inverted shape of the yield curve. For each day under review, this leads to a system of three equations with three known interest rates and three coefficients to be determined. Using this information gives an estimation for the 14-day market interest rate which is applied in the examinations:

$$i(t) = a + b\frac{1}{\sqrt{t}} + c\sqrt{t} \qquad \text{with t = 1, 30, 90 days}$$

Results showing the relation between interest rate advantage and participation, classified by subperiod and type of tender, are shown in *Figures 3-6:*

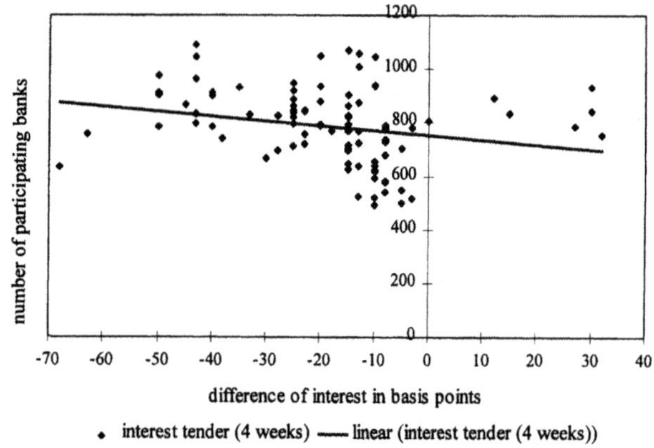

Fig. 3. Number of participating banks versus interest advantage

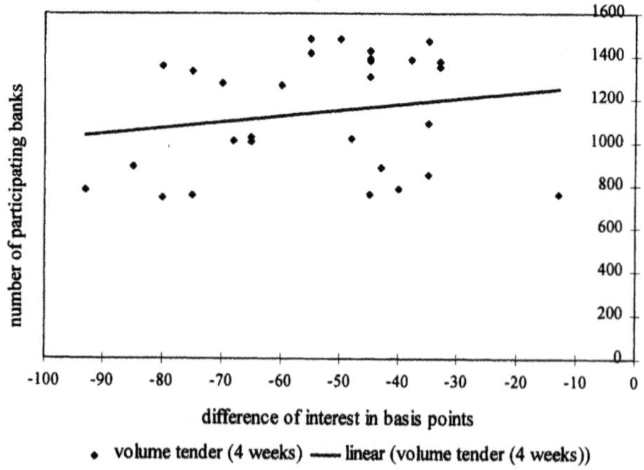

Fig. 4. Number of participating banks versus interest advantage

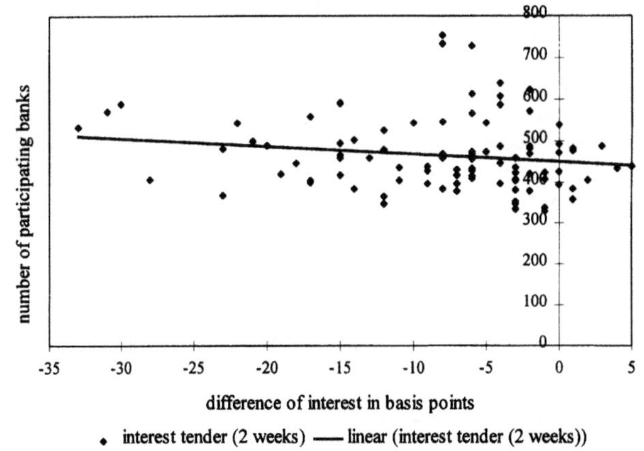

Fig. 5. Number of participating banks versus interest advantage

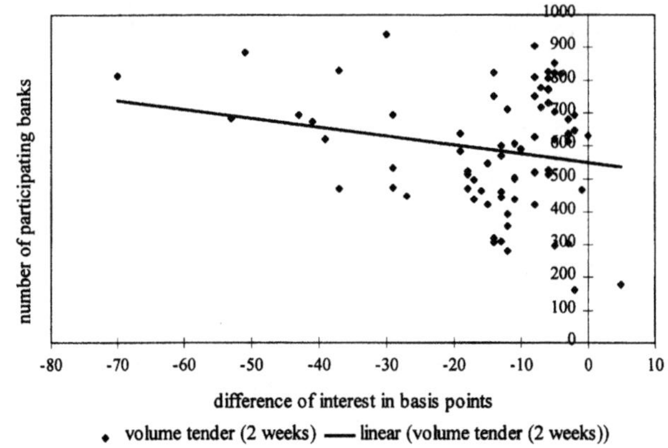

Fig. 6. Number of participating banks versus interest advantage

- It becomes apparent that in a vast majority of cases, the interest rate offered in SRTs is below the respective market rate. The distribution of interest rate advantages is also of interest.
- On an aggregated basis, Menkhoff (1996a) observed a positive relation between the degree of interest rate advantage and participation. This is roughly confirmed by the disaggregated information provided here. Statistical correlations show this relationship to be quite robust in three out of the four cases under review (see *Table 10*).

Table 10. Interest rate advantage of SRTs and participation

	8.1988-9.1992		10.1992-1.1996	
	Volume tender	Interest tender	Volume tender	Interest tender
General information				
Number of events*	29	95	72	96
Average repo rate	6.716	8.026	5.771	5.943
Average money market rate	7.251	8.212	5.918	6.022
Difference (repo - market)	-0.535	-0.186	-0.147	-0.079
Linear regression				
Const.	1282.41	752.16	550.34	450.30
(significance T-value)	*(0.000)*	*(0.000)*	*(0.000)*	*(0.000)*
Regression coefficient	2.667	-1.822	-2.650	-1.880
(significance T-value)	*(0.330)*	*(0.021)*	*(0.087)*	*(0.094)*
R^2	0.035	0.056	0.041	0.030
Rank correlation				
r_s	0.2049	-0.3742	0.0142	-0.1845
(significance)	*(0.286)*	*(0.000)*	*(0.906)*	*(0.072)*

* Only "standard" tender auctions are considered.

- Volume tenders are usually offered with a larger discount on the market rate than interest rate tenders.
- As only few of the SRTs after 1992 have interest rates above the market rate, and most are close to the respective market rate, this demonstrates that the method chosen for calculating the market rate is

probably not misleading.[16]

In summary, this examination provides empirical evidence to support both propositions under review, i.e. that the characteristic risk incorporated in different kinds of tender types influences the participation of banks, and that the price advantage influences participation. Unfortunately, in the case of volume tenders versus interest rate tenders, both effects are evident. Further work to analyse the participation decisions of banks is therefore worthwhile.

Taking a more general approach, a regression can be tested which includes all proposed variables to explain the degree of participation. These variables are the degree of interest rate advantage in comparison to the respective market rate (ADV), and a dummy indicating whether the SRT is a volume or an interest rate tender (DUM). Finally, there may be an influence from the general tightness of money markets which could be highlighted by introducing a third variable, such as the interest rate level (LEV).

The result for both subperiods is shown in *Table 11.*

Table 11. Factors explaining participation with SRTs

Period	CONST	ADV	DUM (i.t.=1;v.t.=0)	LEV	R^2
8.1988-9.1992	1049.5	-82.0	-330.9	6.4	*0.421*
T-value	9.6	-0.9	-6.7	0.6	
Significance	*(0.000)*	*(0.366)*	*(0.000)*	*(0.579)*	
10.1992-1.1996	628.6	-324.9	-100.9	-14.7	*0.227*
T-value	15.5	-3.2	-4.7	-2.1	
Significance	*(0.000)*	*(0.002)*	*(0.000)*	*(0.034)*	
8.1988-9.1992	1101.1	-71.8	-328.4	-	*0.420*
T-value	19.1	-0.8	-6.7	-	
Significance	*(0.000)*	*(0.417)*	*(0.000)*	-	
10.1992-1.1996	553.9	-241.9	-107.8	-	*0.205*
T-value	26.4	-2.5	-5.0	-	
Significance	*(0.000)*	*(0.012)*	*(0.000)*	-	

[16] Taking the overnight interest rate instead of the 14-day money market rate does not change the picture.

The regression analysis shows that the dummy factor in all cases under review has highly significant explanatory power. Although the interest rate advantage is important in the second subperiod, it does not provide any new explanation of the other factors during the first subperiod (this is hardly surprising in the light of the data in Figure 4). Similarly, the interest rate level only becomes important in the second subperiod. Although there are four significant factors for the later period, including the constant term, the R^2 is even lower than in the first subperiod. This indicates that there are other important factors for participation decisions. It is not clear ex ante whether these other influences are at all systematic. Bearing this in mind, the regression demonstrates the high importance of the type of tender for the participation decision of banks.

If this result is integrated into the line of argument in this section, the result is that the statistically significant preference of banks for the volume tender is seen as evidence for the importance of information and institutional characteristics for participation. If smaller banks are less qualified in this respect, as has been assumed, SRTs have an influence on competition between banks. The question of whether this influence is meaningful in an economic sense requires further information about the advantages of participation.

Rough calculations following this direction show that the advantage of SRT interest rates below market level multiplied by SRT volumes leads to a "subsidy" of around DM 60 to 90m being distributed only among those banks participating in SRTs (for details see Menkhoff, 1996a). Besides the supposed size effect, as discussed above, there is also an asset structure effect: those banks with a greater share of securities have a comparatively higher basis for their bids. In summary, although SRTs offer a better basis for fair competition than, for example, rediscount credits, SRT practice means that they are not genuinely fair at present.

3.3.5 Securities repurchase transactions: questionnaire analysis

The preceding section demonstrated the advantage of having hard facts about the effective use of securities repurchase transactions (SRTs) by German banks. In particular, there is no quantitative information about whether participation is systematically related to the institutional characteristics of banks. As the Bundesbank too was unable to produce this information, a questionnaire analysis was conducted to improve the available data.

In terms of balance sheet volume, the most important German banking group is the savings banks, accounting for a market share of around 20% and representing about 16% of all institutions (600 out of 3,700 at the end of 1995). As the range between the smallest and the largest savings bank is roughly a factor of 100, these banks form a reasonable basis to extract a sample for the questionnaire. To ensure a high response rate the *Wissenschaftsförderung der Sparkassenorganisation* (an association established by the German savings banks to promote research in the fields of banking and economics), undertook to send the questionnaires to the individual savings banks and collect the answers. All completed questionnaires were presented to the researcher in anonymous form. To make the questionnaire as understandable as possible, several interviews with savings banks were conducted in advance.

A total of 120 savings banks were approached on 8 May 1996. To improve the chances of a representative response, all savings banks were assigned to six groups, each containing roughly the same number of banks by balance sheet volume. Within each group, a random sample was addressed, and the sample was split again in two smaller groups within the group with the biggest volume.

Table 12. Information about questionnaire and response

Balance sheet volume in DM bn	Mailed questionnaires	Response	Response rate	Number of savings banks
< 0.5	16.6%	13.6%	60%	11.6%
0.5 - 1	16.6%	17.0%	75%	19.6%
1 - 1.5	16.6%	14.8%	65%	18.1%
1.5 - 2	16.6%	13.6%	60%	14.1%
2 - 3	16.6%	21.6%	95%	15.7%
3 - 4.5	8.3%	9.1%	80%	10.3%
> 4.5	8.3%	10.2%	90%	10.6%
Total	120	88	73%	623

The response period was limited until the 24 May 1996. All questionnaires received by the end of May were considered, with those arriving later ignored. The overall response within the period described was 88 questionnaires, giving a response rate of 73.3%. A comparison of the structure of the sample taken with the structure of the respondent banks shows that the response sample is roughly representative with respect to savings bank size (for details see *Table 12*; comprehensive information on the questionnaire and its results is provided by Menkhoff, 1996b).

In terms of the potentially relevant institutional characteristics of the savings banks, questions focused on money market activity in addition to bank size. As the correlation between size and the other proxies is very high, a distinction in bank size in the following examination is justified to keep the arguments as simple as possible.

In terms of the relative importance of SRTs in comparison with the rediscount facility, the evidence strongly supports the qualitative impression expressed in the earlier sections:

- 86 out of 88 respondents use the rediscount facility, demonstrating that this is a widely-used instrument.
- 83 out of the total of 88 savings banks have the custody account necessary to participate in SRTs.
- Only 67 savings banks, however, say that they ever participate in the Bundesbank's open market auctions. The degree of participation is strongly correlated to the size of the respondents as *Figure 7* shows.
- Reviewing only the 59 respondents which use both instruments (and which gave an answer), the average quantitative importance of SRTs was 55%. This figure increases continuously by savings bank size, starting with 10% for the smallest group of banks, 38% for the next group and rising to 62% for the largest savings banks. The average figure is an overestimation of the true share, as about 20 further banks use only the rediscount facility. In terms of volumes, however, the proportion would be considerably higher because of the higher weighting of the larger savings banks.

Another issue which was examined in the last section and which required further empirical substantiation is the preference for volume or interest rate tenders.

In this respect, the preferences revealed by the responding savings banks are the same as for all banks in Germany, as shown by the answers on participation at nine defined auctions: volume tenders receive higher participation rates than interest rate tenders. Taking this detailed information about participation at auctions together with the broader information presented above, a picture emerges of four categories of banks with regard to their use of SRTs:

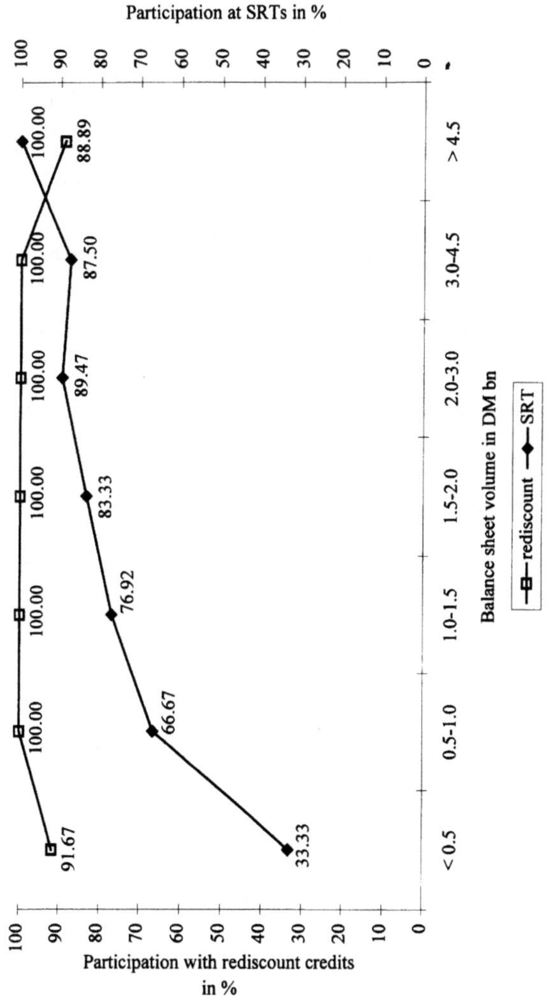

Fig. 7. Participation with rediscount credit and SRTs

- The top category are almost permanent users of SRTs. These are the larger banks, which may for example be savings banks with a total balance sheet volume of more than DM 4.5bn. They make up roughly 5% of all German banks.
- The upper middle category are frequent users of SRTs. These are banks in the range of about DM 1bn to DM 4.5bn asset volume. They represent roughly 15% of all banks.
- The lower middle category are infrequent users of SRTs. These are typically banks with assets below DM 1bn. Further calculations about transaction costs and average interest advantage from participation in SRTs show that there is a minimum bank size for economically profitable participation in auctions. This is probably somewhere in the region of DM 400m (Menkhoff, 1996b). As this threshold value depends on several parameters, the concrete lower limit for this category of banks may be around DM 300 or 200m. This translates into a possible 30% of banks falling into this category.
- The bottom category typically do not use SRTs at all. The somewhat arbitrarily derived threshold value of DM 250m covers the smallest 50% of German banks.

3.3.6 Conclusions

A summary of the competition policy analysis of the three key monetary policy instruments shows a clear picture for the situation in Germany today, but only in this context: securities repurchase transactions come closest to the ideal - but with minor restrictions as things stand today - as far as fair competition is concerned. Minimum reserves and rediscount quotas pose greater problems; although their nature means they can never be perfect, they can still come close to ensuring fair competition.

In this initial scenario, the reduced quantitative importance of the latter two instruments is a valuable contribution to ensuring fair competition. As in most industrialized nations, lower reserve ratios in Germany and the growing importance of open market policy have brought some progress here in terms of competition policy. However, there is still room for improvement, which could best be utilized by fixing interest rates for rediscount credits (or: lending facilities) and for the (partial) remuneration of reserve requirements at near-market rates. For incentive reasons, however, these should remain slightly below the market rates. For instance, one could imagine these rates at a few tenths of a percentage point below the repo rate.

Moreover, it is the author's opinion that the method of calculating these instruments should be reviewed for theoretical reasons. As long as liquidity cushioning is seen as the function of minimum reserves, their orientation towards the volume of payments appears worthy of examination. As long as one has a restriction in liquidity in mind, the Dutch example, which addresses both functions by separate measures, would be consistent. For the second purpose, it is linked to growth in the volume of credit, in other words a reserve requirement on increases in assets. Finally, the award of refinancing quotas will always imply a certain element of subsidy to ensure that the volume is utilized in full. In the author's opinion, fair distribution should be linked to the sole commodity common to all institutions in the production of banking services: capital.

If the reform of minimum reserve requirements and refinancing policy is pursued to the extent proposed here (low reserve requirement ratios, interest paid on compulsory reserves, near-market refinancing rate, and possible changes to the methods of calculation), distortion of competition will be minimized. However, this would see greater exposure of the - currently minor - competition policy weaknesses of open market policy.

3.4 Analysis of decentralization

3.4.1 Uniformity and subsidiarity

It has already been stated in the introduction that the goal of decentralized monetary policy can only be pursued if three basic conditions are fulfilled:

- Firstly, it should be subordinated to efficiency if doubts arise.
- Secondly, implementation should not be associated with industrial policy measures, because goal conflicts could then arise all too easily.
- Thirdly, implementation of monetary policy must be uniform in all regions of the currency area.

Although these basic conditions - which correspond to the consensus - exclude some factors, they provide no positive definition of which instruments should be used in what way. The requirement of uniformity in particular results in tension with the principle of subsidiarity stipulated in treaties and agreements. This is the case at least if subsidiarity is put into more concrete form, because this does not only address organizational levels, but also deliberately permits differences in institutions between and in the countries of monetary union. Such diversity may be desirable not only for political reasons, but also because it forms a fruitful institutional basis for competition and innovations. In this respect, decentralization can most certainly be seen as promoting growth in the longer term (see Vanberg, 1992, for more details).

A careful distinction should be made, however, between this argument and the concept of selective encouragement of diversity. In the field of economics, subsidiarity in the sense described above means above all that there should be no discrimination against institutions (as an extended term for conditions, including processes, etc.), whilst subsidiarity in the sense of promoting diversity can mean that some structures may be deliberately preserved, for example because they have always differed from country to country. From an economic perspective, such a notion is untenable because it stands in the way of open structural change.

On the other hand, the concept of subsidiarity outlined above goes beyond fair competition. This is evident in the organization of public institutions such as the ECB, because the smallest entities possible should be involved in decision-making. However, it also applies to the organization of the basic framework for private competition. Whereas a concrete understanding of fair competition could boil down to equitable competition between existing competitors or processes, subsidiarity demands that specific attention must be paid to ensuring that the relevant institutions continue to operate or can be established.

To put it in a nutshell, there is broad agreement that subsidiarity cannot allow any limitations on management efficiency in the field of monetary policy, although a certain degree of restriction on cost efficiency may be allowed. If subsidiarity is a positive principle, then its implementation may cost something. It is conceded that this position is debatable, not so much in Germany, but elsewhere in Europe. If, however, subsidiarity is always subordinated to the goal of efficiency, then it becomes rather meaningless, something which seems to be appreciated by several proponents. As a measure of the implementation of this goal, the criterion of decentralization will be analysed for monetary policy instruments in greater detail below. This starts with the overall framework imposed by the authorities (3.4.2), continues with financing structures (3.4.3) and moves on to the internal organization of the ECB (3.4.4).

3.4.2 Which financial sector structures are worth preserving?

The question of which financial sector structures are worth preserving is not at all meant rhetorically, as could be implied from the previous section. From an economic point of view, nothing which is clearly inefficient or which distorts competition should be preserved. However, there may well be an area where there are options characterized by a greater or lesser degree of decentralization. Three approaches will be analysed as empirically quantifiable indicators of decentralization:

- The size of institutions, because one can assume that as a rule, decentralization increases as size decreases;
- The diversity of bank locations, because it can be expected that more locations will do better justice to the criterion of decentralization;
- Organizational diversity, because completely different forms of organization may reflect decentralization more strongly than a single organizational form.

1. Size of institutions

The question here is which monetary policy instruments will suit the possibly specific requirements of smaller institutions, provided that these institutions are efficient? If they cannot compete on their own strength, monetary policy does not have to make allowances for this as well.

There are theoretically conflicting influences on the relationship between institutional size and efficiency. On the one hand, larger entities unquestionably benefit from economies of scale, but on the other, large organizational units are subject to specific complexity costs. In purely theoretical terms, there is therefore little that can be said about what constitutes an optimum corporate size, but with one qualification: for all banking services, there are minimum sizes that must be achieved for efficient production. However, these minimum sizes vary depending on the task involved. It is probably very small for standard deposit operations, but evidently very large for foreign operations on an international scale.

This task-related diversity is also the problem in empirical studies examining the relationship between size and efficiency, because they do not distinguish sufficiently between company-specific objectives (as this information is difficult to classify). In other words, such examinations are cross-sectional studies of more or less homogeneous numbers of banks. Their results are very uniform: there appears to be no clear size-related differences in efficiency, with the exception of inefficient micro-operations (see overviews in Berger et al., 1993; Boyd et al., 1993; Tichy, 1990).

Although this cannot be of much specific help to bank management for the methodological problems outlined above, it is a useful indication from a macroeconomic perspective that existing competitors can be competitive almost irrespective of their size. In terms of the instruments studied here and the goal of subsidiarity, this means that although the (design of the) instruments should not promote small institutions, it should treat them fairly, even if this is somewhat cost-intensive for the central bank.

2. Diversity of locations

Of the three structural characteristics under investigation here, the diversity of locations undoubtedly has the closest direct link to the goal of decentralization. This in turn has at least two aspects, namely comprehensive branch network coverage and the multiplicity of more important financial centres within each economic region. The question arises of whether a government should promote the extensive provision of banking services in an economic region, and whether monetary policy instruments should take this into account.

Branch density (e.g. the number of branches per 100,000 inhabitants) - a factor which will also serve here as an indicator of distribution - varies widely in Europe, with Germany ranging at the upper end of the density scale. The problem in terms of welfare economics is to establish the optimum branch density and whether this is identical on a cross-border basis. In the author's opinion, economics cannot supply an answer to this type of question, because preferences and willingness to assume costs cannot be established reliably from a macro-economic viewpoint. In terms of economics, however, it can be said that provided there is functioning competition, a branch will also be established if users can bear its costs, in other words that it is worthwhile in terms of marginal analysis. Moreover, one must accept any political consensus which may be reached and which might aim for a particular level of branch availability (see Kirchgässner, 1993, for the general argument).

The problem involving the number of financial centres in a large country is very similar. Again, there cannot be any specific number from the economist's viewpoint, but only an indication of the result of competition processes. In the opinion of some observers, the debate about the future of the eight stock exchanges in Germany shows quite clearly that certain interests not driven by macroeconomic rationality are involved, and that these are obstructing competition (e.g. Jochimsen, 1993).

The advocates of a large number of financial centres believe that this will have a similar knock-on effect on the number of jobs, in other words positive agglomeration, whilst the supporters of increased centralization draw attention to the advantages to be gained in an international competitive environment. These lines of argument essentially demonstrate that in fact this does not necessarily involve a contradiction, but rather - from an economic perspective - involves competitive roles in a competitive environment (Pagano/Roell, 1990, tend towards this view). There are signs that in future, smaller stock markets will no longer offer a full range of products, because some operators depend on volumes which these markets cannot offer. On the other hand, apart from a generally desirable competition between several financial centres, there are advantages in regional specialization which could justify not only more, but also smaller marketplaces (see Schmidt, 1992). In concrete terms, institutional investors in Germany will - for rational reasons - prefer Frankfurt, which will then compete with London, whilst small investors interested in regional securities could well prefer evolving structures in Hamburg, Munich, etc.

From an economic point of view, the "solution" is firstly not to ignore structural change, and secondly to prevent particular groups of market operators from acting in self-interest by forcing through institutions which unnecessarily obstruct market access for others. Similar to the issue of branch density, competition could lead to changes (possibly in the direction of greater specialization than in the past), but these are unlikely to be known to the authorities in advance.

There are no economically conclusive pointers towards inferable optimum parameters for either branch density or financial centres (stock markets in this instance). This applies to both directions, so that in concertation with subsidiarity concepts, monetary policy instruments should ensure that there can be a multiplicity of economically feasible locations, possibly with specific functions.

3. Organizational diversity

Finally, the third indicator of decentralization which can be enlisted is the organizational diversity of banking institutions, always assuming that any special local needs are expressed in this diversity. As far as Germany is concerned, this means the savings banks and cooperative banks restricted to particular regions.

As with the two previous indicators of decentralization, one can also hold that this is a political task, which is why it should not be the responsibility of a central bank to steer it with its monetary policy tools. However, it is understandable that a central bank should wish to take the potential macroeconomic costs and benefits of such targets into account when taking its essentially independent decision on how to design its monetary policy instruments. This study becomes relevant if allowance for decentralization results in impairment to the quality of the financial system.

Consistent with the goal of subsidiarity, one can assume that institutions with a restricted, regional operating area are in a better position to do justice to the requirements of decentralization than supraregional institutions with a branch network. Apart from potentially more motivated staff due to local loyalties, there is above all the forced concentration of business activities on a particular, unenlargeable economic area. The effect of this is that these institutions orient their business policy to the economic development of this area out of pure self-interest. From an economic viewpoint, this positive effect, a result of pressure to exhaust market potential, may be offset in borderline cases by the fact that resources are allocated for most profitable utilization in a single, limited area. However, this is a marginal view, because alternative investments on the financial markets, combined with the profit motive of the credit institutions, prevent what could otherwise be the potential squandering of capital. A careful consideration of the importance of these external effects would require considerably more detailed study.

However, it may be the case that not even the exhaustion of potential - desired by regional policy - is the economically relevant reason for the existence of the locally limited institutions, but rather that because of their information advantage as local specialists, and their possibly quicker decisions due to local concentration "...the specific knowledge at these institutions of local economic conditions, and direct personal contact between customers, corporate management and their principal bank, are all contributory factors to the lowering of information and transaction costs" (Deutsche Bundesbank, 1994b, own translation). From this perspective, the organization of regionally focused institutions would be less the result of regional policy objectives than the exploitation of a specialization advantage, which is also less susceptible to disintermediation than, for example, business with multinational enterprises (see Mayer/Vives, 1993, p. 10). In this context, it is also striking that the regional institutions - regardless of their extended product offerings together with associated financial institutions - tend to offer another, more traditional and simpler product range, and do this at a lower cost.

The existence of savings and cooperative banks is not decisive for monetary policy, irrespective of whether their specific corporate mission corresponds to the owners' intentions, or because they are institutions with a market-oriented specialization. What is important in the first instance is the awareness that these regionally operating institutions are obviously by and large competitive.

Another question to be asked is whether the organizational diversity of private, public and cooperative institutions may produce another positive, external effect on the financial system in that this diversity has a stabilizing effect in the event of shocks. In this context, two contradictory effects should be noted. On the one hand, diversity favours stability because the impact of shocks may be felt by the entities in the system with different levels of intensity. On the other hand, the diversity means that shocks may concentrate more heavily on one group in the system, which makes it - and ultimately the overall system - more susceptible to instability.

For example, if one wished to examine whether the competition between the three groups mentioned above is a contributory factor to the high level of stability (measured against the international environment) in the German financial system, other factors would have to be vectored into the analysis. The first of these would have to be banking supervision law, which is regarded as relatively strict in Germany, as well as far-reaching, gradual liberalization against a background of stable macroeconomic conditions.

To summarize this section, the current level of knowledge would tend to support the suggestion that regionally operating institutions viewed as desirable under the principle of subsidiarity do not display any critical external effects for the economy in the current financial system. Above all, they take advantage of a specific specialization advantage which should be taken into consideration in the instruments of monetary policy.

4. Consequences for monetary policy instruments

The previous considerations of financial sector structures and their relationship with decentralization give the impression that there is very little justification for an active policy of preserving the present structures (neither can this decision lie with the responsibility of a central bank). The reason for this is not in any lack of efficiency and the consequent economic rejection of decentralization structures, but rather in its competitiveness.

Empirical studies tend to demonstrate undiminished profitability even at smaller banks, as well as showing that there are also good grounds for the co-existence of several financial centres and that regional institutions are efficient. However, this competitiveness is probably always based on appropriate specialization, so that structures will probably change over time. If products change, the economically feasible minimum operating size could shift up or down (even in both directions simultaneously depending on the operating area), financial centres could satisfy changes in specific requirements and regional institutions will probably frequently redefine their competitive role.

Because there is this process of change, the authorities should not "specify" any current characteristics of existing financial sector structures. On the contrary, it must be ensured that sufficient room for manoeuvre is retained in the competitive environment to allow the character of existing institutions to be modified or redefined. How can this be transferred to the instruments of monetary policy?

In the author's opinion, the crucial factor is to treat smaller institutions - and at the same time, rural and regional institutions, which may not be identical - in the same way as large institutions to the greatest possible extent. Specifically, this means direct and similarly intensive access to central bank money supply. Of the instruments analysed in this study, refinancing policy best meets this requirement. However, it should not be based on commercial bills for this purpose, but on a broad range of instruments. Furthermore, compared with large institutions, smaller ones enjoy a stronger position the less frequently the central bank operates on the money market, dominated as it is by the large institutions. This supports the concept of a minimum reserve requirement with the purely technical function of a liquidity cushion.

Another aspect which should be mentioned at this point is that the geographically widespread availability of currency also contributes to the goal of decentralization. However, it must be assumed that institutions servicing less populated areas will incur higher transaction costs to supply branches and ATMs with cash. In other words, currency holdings cannot be adapted so efficiently to fluctuating demand as when transmission routes are shorter (between the main branches and from the bank to the relevant Land Central Bank). This means that the location of a bank has an impact on its cash management costs which can hardly be said to result from "operational reasons" (Meister/Hofmann, 1994, p. 212). Where a geographically widespread provision, which is in the interests of decentralization, causes higher costs, this should be compensated for. One possibility of doing so would be to deduct vault cash from the minimum reserve requirement (on a pro rata basis), provided that the minimum reserve represents a burden. This sort of arrangement applies in the USA which - not by chance - has an extremely decentralized financial system.

A monetary policy instrument design geared to decentralization is just as efficient in terms of management as one which is restricted to open market policy. In terms of cost efficiency it is probably slightly inferior, but it discriminates less against those institutions whose existence is an indicator of relatively greater decentralization, and thus of subsidiarity.

3.4.3 Implications of idiosyncratic financing structures

The financial systems in Europe have grown over centuries. Differences between countries occur not only with respect to more or less decentralized financial sector structures, such as discussed in the preceding section (3.4.2), but also with respect to idiosyncratic financing structures. The aspect of decentralization here is not one of local diversity, but rather of national divergence. The discussion will cover three steps: firstly, the importance of financing structures in the financial system for monetary policy transmission, secondly, empirical insights into this transmission and, thirdly, consequences for monetary policy instruments.

1. Financing structures and monetary policy transmission

In a generic approach, several characteristics of financing structures can be identified which are potentially relevant for the transmission process of monetary policy. Most generally, issues of organization, maturity, source of finance and velocity of money can be distinguished (see also *Figure 8*):

- As regards the *organizational aspects* of financial sectors, some characteristics have already been discussed above. When it comes to financing, another organizational characteristic becomes important: the issue of bank-based versus market-based financial systems. In Europe, the United Kingdom is seen as a typical market-based system, whereas Germany is representative of the bank-based systems (see e.g. Frankel/Montgomery, 1991). This distinction between two types may be an oversimplification, however, when policy recommendations should be based on it. Breig (1996), for example, demonstrates the way in which several continental European bank-based systems differ from each other. This should not be a surprise, if one bears in mind the heterogeneity in instrumental sets found in this group of central European countries.

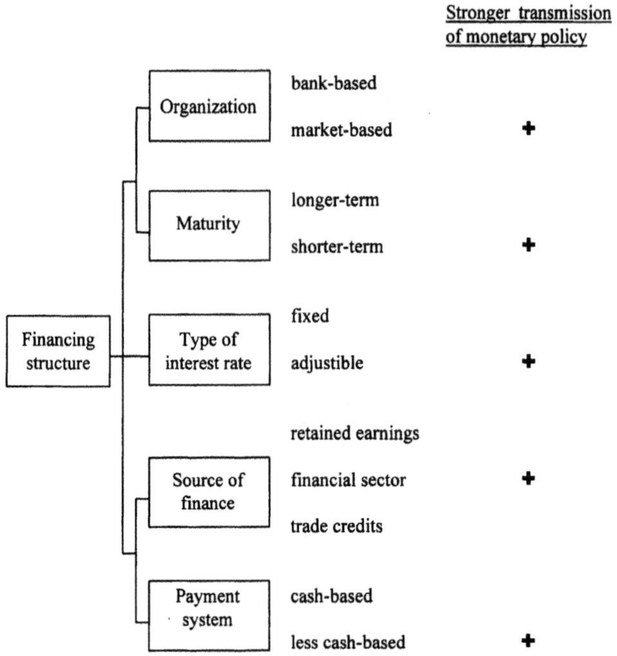

Fig. 8. Financing structure and monetary policy transmission

- The average or typical *maturity* for financing contracts in European countries is probably less influenced by historic developments than by the chosen course of monetary policy. In 1993, low-inflation countries such as Germany and the Netherlands had the highest proportion of medium and long-term credit to the private sector, namely 84% and 83% respectively (Bockelmann, 1996, p.15). Southern European countries with higher inflation rates, however, had lower proportions, for example Italy and Spain with only 49% and 60%.

- The difference is even more pronounced than these figures show, as the *type of interest rate* is related to the maturity. The second group mentioned above has typically adjustable interest rates for longer-term contract, whereas fixed interest rates dominate in the first group (Bockelmann, 1996, p.18).
- The proportion of several sources of finance for enterprises differs not only according to the cyclical state of the economy, but also from country to country. Generally, retained earnings are often the most important source. Within external finance, the importance of securities markets varies markedly (see the organizational characteristic above). It should also be noted that in some countries, such as France and to some degree Spain, trade credit is a relevant source of finance (see Bockelmann, 1996, p.28; Breig, 1996).
- Finally, the *payment system* differs between countries. The relative degree of use of cash for payment transfers has an impact on monetary policy.

There is no doubt that these financing structure idiosyncrasies can influence the behaviour of the financial sector and thus constrain the transmission of monetary policy impulses. Assuming the preference of central banks for dominating the money market as much as possible, the following characteristics of the five distinguished aspects would probably improve the power of central bank actions:

- Market-based systems leave less room for banks to compensate for monetary policy stimuli than bank-based systems.
- The interest rates of shorter-term maturity assets or liabilities are closer to central bank rates. A greater influence can therefore be expected.
- The same applies to a higher share of adjustable rates which reduce the sluggishness of interest rate changes.
- In terms of the sources of finance, monetary policy most directly influences conditions in the financial sector and less, in particular, financing via retained earnings.
- Payment systems in which the proportion of cash-based transactions is low increase the velocity of money and thus decrease the central bank money base required for payment transfer purposes. The smaller the base, the more marginally the actions of the central bank are felt in the money market.

2. Empirical examinations of the relevance of the financing structure for transmission

The amount of empirical research undertaken to examine the effect of financing structure on the monetary transmission mechanism is rather small. More recent work has been provided by the IMF (Cottarelli/Kourelis, 1994, Cottarelli/Ferri/Generale, 1995) and by the BIS (surveyed by Bockelmann, 1996).

The IMF studies, covering industrial and developing countries, address stickiness in bank lending rates compared with money market rates and establish several influences emanating from the financial structure (Cottarelli/Kourelis, 1994, pp. 613 ff.):

- Higher competition between banks, and in particular the elimination of barriers to setting up new branches, tends to reduce the stickiness of bank lending rates.
- A lower proportion of state-controlled banks has the same effect on stickiness.
- The same applies to a lower level of capital controls, although the significance of this effect is dubious.
- The development of a market for short-term instruments also tends to reduce stickiness.
- Finally, less volatile market rates help to reduce stickiness. In general, larger money markets may be expected to reduce volatility in money market prices.

The general message from these examinations seems to be that a more market-oriented financial structure narrows the gap between lending rates and market rates, and thus improves the power of monetary policy.

The empirical work of the BIS, concentrating on industrial countries, investigates the importance of financial structures in three ways (Bockelmann, 1996, pp. 22 ff.):

- In a similar fashion to the IMF studies, it examined the speed and strength at which strong short-term lending rates move in the same direction as the short-term money market rate instrument of monetary policy. The reaction depends on the degree of short-term refinancing of banks: the link is strong in the UK but looser in Germany (or Japan). In the latter countries, which are also characterized by a comparatively large proportion of enterprise financing by bank credits, the subsequent lending rate response appears downwards later than upwards.

- Based on the econometric models of each central bank, the influence of a higher money market rate on the real economy is measured. A 1% increase in the rate leads to a maximum of 0.9% GDP deviation for the UK, but deviations around 0.5% and lower for the continental European countries. The main channel for transmission is the effect on the cost of capital for investment.
- To check for possible differences in the construction of the national models, the calculations were repeated with a similar methodology for all countries. In effect the results became much more similar for the countries although not identical (see in this vein also Gerlach/Smets, 1995).

The message from the BIS stresses the importance of short-term versus long-term financing contracts. A higher proportion of short-term financing enhances the power of monetary policy. Comparing the final outcomes of monetary policy, one would expect that the UK experience is more satisfying than the German one which is, however, not really the case.

3. Consequences for monetary policy instruments

As the theoretical ex ante-consideration and the empirical evidence provide a quite similar picture, it might be tempting to suggest a kind of optimal environment for a powerful central bank. The design of the instruments could be used to give preference to those structures which come closest to the target environment. A consequence of this would be a trend towards the unification of European financing structures. This approach, however, far exceeds the mandate of the ECB.

The most general consequence of the discussion above is to recognize that idiosyncratic national structures may bring out different results from an identical European monetary policy. This may be more important for strategy than for the instruments, but it should probably not be ignored for the latter.

In the longer run, this problem may start disappearing as the structures of financial systems become more similar over time. This will be enforced by harmonization in many fields such as banking supervision, capital markets regulation and so on. One may expect that a uniform regulatory framework and European-wide competition will lead to (more) similar outcomes regarding institutional products:

- To the extent that inflation differences are responsible for the respective maturity of financing contracts, the identical ECB monetary

policy enforces similar inflation rates in the EMU zone and thus an assimilation of maturities.
- The same could happen in the case of payment transfer technology.
- Even regarding the issue of bank-based versus market-based financial systems some advantages of universal banks seem to be acknowledged on the one hand, and e.g. German universal banks become more market-oriented than before on the other hand.

To return to the field of monetary policy instruments, there is an obvious link between financing structures and instruments, i.e. that instruments must be based on financial contracts which are typical for the respective financing structure. In the UK, money market paper is the core asset for instruments. This paper did not exist historically in Germany, but with bank lending predominating, commercial bills channelled via banks were used as underlying asset. In France, more bank-based credit contracts also fulfilled the use of the necessary underlying asset. Therefore, the clear consequence is, to allow for variety in the admissible assets which are used for monetary policy instruments.

In the shorter-term, it can be imagined that the national central banks will retain some discretion on the exact definition on admissible assets. This would also help to reduce the costs of transformation. A tendency towards convergence is already evident today, however, with the UK and Germany again serving as convenient examples:

- Some years ago, the Bundesbank abandoned its strict reservation against any kind of short-term money market paper, and in 1996, even the German government started issuing notes with maturities of less than one year. These later issues are often regarded as a precondition for monetary policy based on money market paper.
- In the UK happens the respective step towards convergence as repurchase transactions with longer-term issues become more common in monetary policy.

3.4.4 A decentrally organized central bank

This section will examine the question of the contribution which the organization of the ECB can make to the goal of decentralization. A certain framework has already been established, in that the overall system of a European Central Bank has been designed as a network of national central banks plus a central institution, the ECB itself. However, the body in which the national central banks are represented is always the one which takes decisions (see Chapter 2.3).

In contrast to the organizational structure, no decisions have yet been made on the organizational processes. However, the organizational structure and the principle of subsidiarity point clearly to the direction "that in the monetary policy of the ESCB, all tasks which are properly performed by the national central banks shall also be transferred to them" (Treutler, 1992, p. 16). The question of what these tasks are will be examined in two stages: the fundamental suitability of the instruments will be discussed, followed then by the room for manoeuvre in the implementation of monetary policy.

As regards suitability for decentralized management, all instruments are subject to a degree of tension: on the one hand, the structures must be uniform, but on the other, elements of management will almost always devolve to decentralized agencies. This is likely to occur most with refinancing policy, because all processing of fixed quotas will be handled by decentralized agencies, i.e. at national central bank level and below. According to Koebnick, "The standing facilities correspond to the principle of subsidiarity more than any other instrument" (Koebnick, 1994). Minimum reserves will also be held in the accounts of the relevant national central bank, and verification of compliance with guidelines and regulations will be undertaken at this level as well.

Seen in these terms, however, open market policy does not depart very much from the other two instruments, because invitations to tender and account-based settlement, for instance for securities repurchase transactions, are handled in Germany by the Land Central Banks. In the author's opinion, however, coordination of the activities of the national central banks will present problems, and final liquidity adjustment will probably be performed centrally (see Monticelli/Viñals, 1993, pp. 21 ff. for further details). However, such "centralized" elements are not inevitable characteristics of the instrument, but rather of its standard utilization today, because - conceptually speaking - a purely refinancing policy would also have to ensure central market adjustment by some means. The consequence of this is that open market policy causes problems for decentralization, above all because it involves an inherent, but not inevitable risk of centralization. To sum up, although refinancing policy and minimum reserves provide more work for the national central banks and their secondary agencies, this is primarily due to the larger overall volume of work; the national agencies do not have more freedom to take decisions.

Whilst the instruments do not reveal much a priori regarding the degree of decentralization which they incorporate, the room for manoeuvre in the implementation of monetary policy may be greater. In his pioneering study, Treutler (1992, pp. 17 ff.) distinguished "four models for the practical implementation of monetary policy in the ESCB" with a varying degree of centralization.[17] Based on the long-standing differences between the countries, the starting point of his analysis is the rejection of complete transfer of particular decision-making structures currently existing at national level to the European level. In particular with the centralist model, this would be "wholly inappropriate, at least in the initial phase" (Treutler, 1992, p. 20). In this model, the national central banks would have no more than purely technical functions in the implementation of monetary policy.

"Instrumental Autonomy" is the opposite of the first model. Under this procedure, the ECB would notify the national central banks of a band for the overnight rate which can be maintained using the variety of national instruments. Treutler addresses the problem of internationally operating institutions migrating to locations with instruments which are attractive to them, concluding that with complete freedom of choice of location and of capital flows, this model would lead to competing instruments (or otherwise to a distortion of competition). If the consequent rejection of particular instruments is to be avoided, they should be harmonized from outset.

The two other models, "Liquidity Autonomy" and "Liquidity Targets", lie mid-way between instrumental autonomy and centralism. The first of these is a toned-down version of instrumental autonomy, with autonomy not covering all instruments but restricted to the calculation of refinancing quotas for refinancing policy. In the latter, national freedom is restricted further in that not only the basic instruments and the overall level of refinancing quotas are stipulated, but also the level of other forms of liquidity supply. The problem of both models is obviously the distortion of competition caused by different national methods of calculating quotas.

With the three comparatively decentralized options for implementation not easy to reconcile with the goal of fair competition, it appears questionable if they are suitable even for a transitional period only. The degree of centralization in monetary policy implementation will have to be as high at European level as it is at national level today. The specific difficulties of the transitional period will therefore have to be solved in other ways:

---

[17] See Treutler, 1992, Annex 3; see also Schulmann, 1994.

- The payment networks for settling central open market operations, which are likely to be inadequate, can be tackled by the greatest possible decentralization of settlement with centralized coordination, in other words with elements of Treutler's Liquidity Target model.
- In a single market, particular national features of the securities on which monetary policy can be based can really only be dealt with in one way: all forms in use must be "approved" everywhere.

To sum up, the organization of the central bank leaves little freedom for genuine decentralization decision-making, over and above decentralization of the sites of the members of the ESCB. Refinancing facilities at uniform conditions correspond most to decentralized concepts, but quota fixing must still be accepted. In terms of implementation, it is conceivable that the national central banks will themselves provide liquidity, including certain open market operations, within a predefined framework, but that market adjustment will be in the hands of the ECB.

The decision-making authority for what should be a unified European monetary policy must ultimately lie centrally with the ECB. The decisive contribution to decentralization will therefore be to influence ECB decisions by allowing the participation of a wide variety of regions - including regional councils - corresponding roughly to the German structure.[18] The current agreement on one representative from each national central bank in the highest decision-making body is a valuable contribution, but with only a few countries involved, it could still be enhanced somewhat, for instance by allowing large countries to nominate two or three representatives to this body. In the case of Germany, representatives of the Land Central Banks would be appropriate.

3.4.5 Conclusions

The options for implementing the principle of subsidiarity in the process of monetary policy decisions, in other words the participation of smaller or lower-ranking entities, such as regions, are very limited. The major contribution would be a decentralized organizational structure for the ECB and the corresponding national central banks. A minor element would be some (temporary) national discretion in the exact definition of which assets are admissible as an underlying guarantee for refinancing or

[18] Not for nothing does Schulmann, 1994, refer to the "Frankfurt Model" in all thoughts on decentralization.

open market policy.

As far as the use of instruments over and above this is concerned, refinancing policy in particular has a slight edge over open market policy (see also Goodhart/Viñals, 1994, p. 178). On the one hand, it ensures direct access to central bank money availability for the smaller institutions and reduces the volumes which have to be channelled onto the market by large institutions. On the other hand, it is comparatively easy for a central bank to implement it decentrally. Decentralization of settlement in the central bank and simplified (but not preferential) decentralization of the commercial banks are thus complementary. In addition, minimum reserves may have certain advantages for decentralized financial systems if they are used as a liquidity cushion to reduce the need for the central bank to intervene in the money market.

Where decentralization is the focus of consideration of the organization of monetary policy instruments in Europe, there is a very clear trend in favour of refinancing policy, albeit more in the form of broadly based standing facilities rather than the rediscounting of commercial bills (see also Goodhart/Viñals, 1994, p. 178). For this reason, it is rather difficult to understand when even advocates of such facilities who explicitly endorse decentralization still concede that this instrument is appreciably inferior to open market policy.[19] On the contrary, the question to be asked is how high the maximum proportion of central bank money provision accounted for by such standing facilities could be, without endangering the efficiency of monetary management.

3.5 Policy options for lending facilities and reserve requirements

The preceding analyses of the three goals of efficiency, fair competition and decentralization showed that there certainly can be a justification for the two critical instruments of lending facilities and minimum reserves. The possible policy options for the design of these two instruments will now be discussed in a comparative overview. The reference base for these overviews are the current German arrangements used throughout this study. Some options stick closely to this starting point, whilst others vary.

The current German lending facilities (Model I) and the reforms proposed by Issing/Rudolph (1988; Model Ia) have already been discussed.

[19] For instance Koebnick, 1994; and similarly Remsperger, 1994a.

Table 13. Alternative models of lending facility arrangements

Model	Description	Distribution of volume	Interest rate	Admissible assets	Documentation in
I	Present German arrangement	Credit-related contingents	Fixed, below market	Trade bills of highest quality	Deutsche Bundesbank (1994a)
Ia	Slightly modified German arrangement	Contingents according to the absolute volume of short-term and medium-term credit	= Model I	= Model I	Issing/Rudolph (1988)
Ib	= Model Ia	= Model I	= Model I	Non-financial transactions related paper of highest quality	Hesse/Braasch (1996)
II	Modified German arrangement	Equity capital-related contingents	Flexible, below market rate (repo rate minus discount)	Broad variety of qualified assets	Menkhoff (1996)
III	Volume tender arrangement	Auction with given interest rate and proportional repartiation	= Model I	= Model Ib	Hesse/Braasch (1996)
IV	Interest tender arrangement	Dutch style auction	Bids are made as repo rate plus / minus margin	= Model II	Menkhoff (1996a)

Section 3.3.2 also contains a justification for a fundamental modification to the current German rediscount credit. This retains the quota and below market interest rate components, but dispenses with a constant discount rate in favour of less subsidy (Model II; cf. *Table 13*).

However, the current discussion both in academic circles and at a political level has shown that there are very strong reservations about all non-market elements, initially irrespective of any justifications there may be. This is probably linked to fundamental reservations concerning political economy. Design proposals have been developed in recent years which retain lending facilities, but burden them with fewer interventionist elements.

In this context, Hesse/Braasch (1996) extended their definition of admissible paper from the classic trade bills to other paper linked to activities in the real economy (Model Ib) as a first stage. In the second stage, they depart from the existing quota arrangement and discuss volume tenders as a method of distribution (model III). The problem with volume tenders, however, as long as they are still offered at relatively attractive interest rates, is that a sort of bidding competition can arise in which the structure of the banks involved can result in competitive differences.

To avoid this – and also to concentrate core monetary policy on a single key interest rate (Model II), there is a further proposal which also dispenses with the two traditional elements of quotas and administered interest rates, following the discussion mentioned above. In addition to the standard SRTs, this envisages another facility whose interest rate would be based on the first one, where bids would be submitted in the form of premiums or discounts on the "normal" repo rate. It is expected that banks with information disadvantages would benefit in particular from this facility. However, they would have to pay a price to avoid transaction costs, i.e. the premium which would probably emerge. Because this is intended to allow above all smaller banks direct access to central bank money supply, the Dutch-style auction would be the most appropriate (Model IV).

The main discussion on lending facilities, based on market conformity, is also reflected in the options for designing minimum reserves. If this monetary policy instrument is based on a certain degree of rationality, a number of options are available compared with the current German arrangements (Model I; see *Table 14* for a comparison). In the first stage of reform, one could image reducing the effective minimum reserve burden still further (following the success in other countries), either by cutting rates further or by reducing the assessment basis (Model IIa).

Table 14. Alternative models of reserve requirement arrangements

Model	Description	Gross burden in % of GDP	Eligible basis	Remuneration	Documentation in
I	Present German arrangement	~ 1	Sight, time, savings	no	Deutsche Bundes-bank (1995)
IIa	Minimizing arrangement	0.1 - 1.0	= model I	no	Diverse sources
IIb	= model IIa	= models I / IIa	= models I / IIa	yes	Diverse sources
III	Voluntary arrangement	?	= models I/II	yes, if preannounced	Remsperger/ Angenendt (1995)
IV	Transactions oriented arrangement	> model II	Volume of payment transfers as basis	Partially	Menkhoff (1996)
V	Functional split arrangement	a) = models II - IV	= models II - IV	= models II - IV	Wellink (1994)
		b) 0+X	e.g. additional credit volume	no	

Perhaps the simplest step in this direction which could be implemented as a supplementary measure would be near-market interest payable on minimum reserves (Model IIb).

In a fundamental variation of this arrangement – typifying today's thinking – there has been a proposal to pay interest only on the voluntary reserves which have been announced (Model III). The underlying intention is to encourage banks to disclose their working balances hidden to the central bank and thereby simplify monetary policy management. The apparent incentive for the banks would be the interest paid on their working balances. From the point of view of the central bank, however, any voluntary concept runs counter to the nature of minimum reserves.

In another fundamental variation on the conventional arrangements, the possibility of linking the basis of assessment for reserves held by individual banks to the volume of their payment transactions could be examined. This concept also requires working balances held by the banks in their own interests. Only the portion by which the minimum reserve requirement exceeds the approximated voluntary balances at the central bank would earn interest (Model IV; see also Section 3.3.1).

Finally, the existing models could be linked to a functional splitting of the reserves held: a "normal" minimum reserve and a supplementary reserve for extreme liquidity expansion similar to the Dutch model. Interest payments on the liquidity constraint could be dispensed with to strengthen the effect of this component (Model V).

For both lending facilities and reserve requirements, the analysis in this chapter shows that the present German situation represents an arrangement which can be ameliorated. In this respect, all the political options presented are improvements on the status quo; they can also be combined in a variety of ways and may be modified further.

4 Discussion of alternative concepts

4.1 Outline

The previous sections analysed the pros and cons of advantageous monetary policy instruments in Europe from a variety of perspectives. Some of these arguments are no longer suited to the situation of the institutions today, but in many cases, the weighting to be attached to controversial positions is also a question of political objectives. To simplify orientation, the continuum of positions which can be formed from combinations of different arguments will be reduced to three key concepts: a "lean", a "conservative" and a "decentralized" concept.

These concepts are neither generally right nor generally wrong, but each of them is cogent in its own right. The difference lies in the assumptions which are made - at least implicitly - about the functioning of the financial system, and consequently in the different priorities which monetary policy must pursue. Such differences do not relate to core views shared by all concepts:

- Monetary policy must be efficient, i.e. in particular it must have control over central bank money creation and over conditions on the money market.
- It should promote the stability of the financial system, although opinions may differ over how this should be implemented in concrete terms.
- Monetary policy should not distort competition or obstruct the principle of subsidiarity.
- Finally, the consensus on the instruments also applies to the three concepts (see Chapter 2.6): a strong role for open market policy, low minimum reserve requirements and refinancing policy as a safety-

valve function.

Beyond this common core, however, monetary policy instruments can be designed very differently and still be efficient. The cross-border comparative study by Bernanke/Mishkin (1993) gives the impression that the specific details of the instruments are not the major factor for achieving monetary policy objectives. Rather, various paths can be followed to achieve the goals. Although this means that one need not be overly concerned about the macroeconomic impact, it is still clear that the three concepts differ substantially in the details.

The proposed terms for these concepts will be the guidelines in this respect (see overview in *Table 15*). The lean concept has lean government as its "sponsor", i.e. it implies the minimum possible intervention, including by monetary authorities, and a correspondingly high level of trust in the efficiency of purely private markets. The counterpoint to this is the conservative concept. Although it does not always assume market failure, it believes that this is possible and thus allocates to national authorities the task of "curing" and stabilizing these negative externalities of private markets. The decentralized concept is not a hybrid of the other two, but a completely separate third view which attaches great importance to the principle of subsidiarity.

That these are stylized concepts is evident from the fact that practically nobody would agree completely with any of these concepts, but would rather propose specific modifications here and there. This can be seen in the example of the Bundesbank, which outlined its policy in its annual report published in 1993 (see Deutsche Bundesbank, 1993, pp. 90 ff.). In its "Reflections on a European monetary concept", the Bundesbank mentions only the instruments of open market policy and minimum reserves, with the latter being reduced to the function of a liquidity cushion.[1] This approach is at odds with the three theoretical concepts, but its emphasis on open market policy, the ignoring of refinancing policy (except for its safety-valve function) and the technical function of minimum reserve requirements, which can hardly be termed a "policy", means that it is probably closest to the lean concept (shown clearly in König, 1994).

There are also elements of the conservative concept, such as the basic incorporation of minimum reserves - intended partly to skim off liquidity - or the proposed integration of commercial bills and other real-economy instruments into open market policy. Finally, elements of decentralization

[1] In contrast, Bundesbank Vice President Gaddum (1994, p. 76) writes of "a check on money creation and a liquidity cushion".

also appear, albeit restricted in this publication to "technical aspects of central bank money provision" (Deutsche Bundesbank, 1993, p. 91). Elsewhere, however, minimum reserves are explicitly justified using the argument of easier decentralization (see Meister/Hofmann, 1994, p. 214; Jochimsen, 1994b). It is possible that at present, the Bundesbank does not have a consistent overall position.

Table 15. Three concepts for monetary policy instruments

Feature	Lean concept	Conservative concept	Decentralized concept
Primary motivation	Efforts to achieve efficiency	Worries about the stability of the financial system	Facilitate decentralization
Assumptions	Inherent stability; limit government influence	Inherent susceptibility to crisis; financial sector as a disruptive factor	Indifferent to stability; to facilitate subsidiarity
Characteristic instrument	Open market policy	Minimum reserves to counter excessive liquidity	Standing facilities
Open market policy	Core instrument	Key quantitive instrument	Covers need for flexibility
Minimum reserves	Superfluous	Restrict liquidity	Liquidity cushion
Refinancing policy	Superfluous	Shields the real economy; targets supply of liquidity in times of crisis	Key to facilitating decentralization
Typical country	UK, Canada	Germany	Elements in the Netherlands
Advocates	Issing, Geiger, Remsperger, monetarists	Hesse, Koebnick, Timmermann, Mishkin (possibly)	Schulmann

Note: The positions outlined above do not necessarily reflect all the opinions of the individuals cited above or the situation in these countries.

4.2 Lean v. conservative concept

Roughly speaking, the opinions on the organization of the array of monetary policy instruments of the future ECB which dominate the literature can be ascribed to the lean or the conservative concept. Both approaches represent more deeply rooted undercurrents of economic theory, and it is therefore not surprising that - at least on the face of it - they are also at odds in this topical question. To understand these competing concepts, it would be helpful to examine these fundamental ideas in greater detail.

The most evident starting point for the background to the lean concept is the closeness of this proposal to monetary policy under optimum conditions (see Chapter 3.1). Indeed, the easiest explanation of the lean concept is that it is based on efficient markets in which the monetary management function is primarily that of controlling the money market. For this single purpose, open market policy is probably the most suitable instrument, and thus the only one worth considering. In contrast, minimum reserves adversely affect private transactions and distort competition. In the lean concept, refinancing policy is a suboptimal instrument due to its longer maturities and elasticity. The United Kingdom surely represents the most prominent example in Europe of this form of monetary policy.

The opposite example is probably Germany, despite a certain degree of catching up, or even a change of course in recent years[2] (see Chapter 2.5 for further details). Traditionally, Germany's central bank has always maintained a particularly strict commitment to stability in all its various aspects, such as price stability and the stability of the financial system.[3] This focus on stability may in itself sharpen sensitivity to possible dangers, which in turn promotes a multi-instrument approach to monetary policy. The greater the variety of means available, the quicker any threats to stability can be countered. Moreover, the emphasis on stability may also imply a relative aversion to experiments. It is inevitable that an innovation may well result in unexpected adjustment reactions on the part of market operators. This could be one of the reasons for the comparatively "old-fashioned" orientation of monetary policy instruments in Germany.

---

[2] For example, former Bundesbank President Schlesinger argued in favour of standing facilities; see Schlesinger, 1992, p. 17

[3] See Bundesbank Directorate member Häusler, 1994, p. 7f; he accuses other central banks of freeriding to support national financial centres, with the stability-oriented Bundesbank picking up the bill.

Because the countries participating in Monetary Union must reach a consensus, there will undoubtedly be a compromise lying somewhere between the purely theoretical forms of the two concepts. For instance, an attempt could be made to design an essentially conservative concept in as lean a way as possible, or supplement a lean concept by some precautionary measures. There is a huge variety of potential hybrids, and the Bundesbank position outlined above merely gives one side's impression of how such a stance could look.

Before taking a closer look at the more likely elements of European agreement in Chapter 4.4, a decentralized concept will first be derived, and the reform proposals elaborated in Chapter 3 will also be integrated into this framework.

4.3 A decentralized concept

The justification of the decentralized concept is based on the notion of a Europe constituted in accordance with the principle of subsidiarity. The focus of efforts in this context is neither on the lean solution nor on concern about the stability of the financial system, but rather on facilitating decentralization. This concept will be presented in two stages, starting with a blueprint which ignores concrete design issues (see Table 15 in Chapter 4.1). The advantage of this is that it corresponds roughly to the level of abstraction presented in the two previous concepts. This will then be followed by integrating more specific, albeit relatively contentious, proposals for reform into the concept.

The decentralized concept is essentially derived from the issues discussed in the analysis of decentralization in Chapter 3.4. This produced an emphasis on standing facilities and the reduction of open market policy to the necessary minimum. This specific reversal of the quantitative proportions of the two instruments fundamentally distinguishes the decentralized concept from the other two concepts. The country most closely approaching this concept is the Netherlands, which has a similar weighting of standing facilities and open market operations.

The quantitative weighting in favour of standing facilities may appear problematic at first glance, because it heavily restricts the central bank's ability to manage the money market. However, Monetary Union would change both the opportunities and the need for more flexible intervention in the money market. Based on the German case for simplicity's sake, and assuming that there was a "mini" Monetary Union - for instance involving Germany, France, Austria, the Netherlands and possibly a couple of other smaller countries - the volumes to be managed by the ECB would at least double over the German reference situation (see *Table 16*). On the other hand, the need for flexibility would probably decrease because in recent years, the greatest strains have come from the EMS. However, an expected EMS II would look quite different, as the weight of the EMU within the EMS II would be very high, which would distribute the burden within the EMU and reduce the need for external intervention.

Table 16. Assets of EU's central banks at the end of 1994

Country	Assets in ECU m.	Cumulated assets in ECU m.
Germany	186 517	186 517
France	101 602	288 119
Austria	23 039	311 158
Netherlands	41 459	352 617
Belgium	24 068	376 685
Luxembourg	365	377 050
Denmark	22 164	399 214
Finland	12 345	411 559
Great Britain	34 570	446 129
Greece	42 940	489 069
Ireland	n.a.	
Italy	179 485	668 554
Portugal	23 143	691 697
Spain	90 415	782 112
Sweden	29 457	811 569
Total	811 569	-

Note: The ECU is calculated with the average exchange rate in december 1994

Source: The different central banks' annual report of 1994

If one were to continue this cautious approach and assume that the policy was to maintain the same absolute volume of highly flexible open market operations conducted by the Bundesbank today, the current German ratio of rediscount credits to securities repurchase transactions could still be reversed from roughly 1 to 2, to 2 to 1 in favour of standing facilities which might replace the more restictive rediscount credits.[4] The more the Monetary Union expands, the share accounted for by the latter could be increased further - with good reason. However, the main issue here is not the details of distribution, but rather only that there is probably still room for manoeuvre, whilst at the same time preserving the efficiency of monetary management.

The core of the decentralized concept will be now be fleshed out by concrete, and probably also rather controversial proposals for its design. Separating these concrete proposals from the concept itself should underline the fact that they are merely a basis for discussion, and prevent any dispute about the details necessarily leading to rejection of the fundamental concept. On the other hand, it will probably be helpful to image a concept in the most concrete of terms. The issues here are the instruments, the nature and management of the underlying securities, the method of calculating the standing facilities, the organization of the minimum reserves and the central bank's interest rates.

1. Prioritization of standing facilities

Standing facilities, or more precisely lending facilities (see Figure 1), are designed to provide commercial banks with a basic supply of central bank money because this option most easily ensures genuinely equal treatment for all institutions regardless of size. When weighing standing facilities against the superior management efficiency offered by open market operations, the ratio of around 2 to 1 proposed above should provide a reference point. No more can be really said until the actual participants in Monetary Union are known, together with the currency reserves, central bank money stock in circulation, etc. The only thing that is certain is that the current proportion of rediscount credits in Germany will be the lower limit for the standing facilities of the ECB.

Another instrument which will ease decentralization is a negligible minimum reserve requirement, to be used as a liquidity cushion to reduce central bank operations on the money market. This would also serve the purpose of preventing any unacceptable imbalance in the role of the large

[4] Assuming that the ECB has twice as much assets as the Bundesbank, the volume of SRTs, for example, would be the same, currency reserves might be doubled and standing facilities quadrupled.

institutions active on the money market compared with the smaller institutions not operating in this area. To complete the picture, it should also be noted that there is no dispute that these three instruments should be supplemented by a "safety-valve function" linked to standing facilities, as well as variations on open market policy as fine-tuning measures.

2. All paper in a single custody account

Implementation could be simplified if the various forms of central bank money provision were to be standardized.[5] In Germany today, securities repurchase transactions, lombard loans and working balances to settle payments are all cleared through a single custody account maintained by the bank at the relevant Land Central Bank.

This could be extended to cover standing facilities. However, these should not be restricted merely to commercial bills, not even to holdings of securities; rather, the banks should be allowed to assign prime receivables from lending transactions, such as is the case in France. The type of collateralization is of secondary importance as long as creditworthiness is ensured. This would allow the same custody account, but not the same paper, to be used for multiple purposes:

- For monetary policy purposes, the greatest volume would be accounted for by lending facilities, which could take the form of a sort of quota-based repurchase transaction on a three-month basis.
- In terms of importance, these would be followed by open market operations, which would probably cover maturities of around two weeks in most cases. The easier it is for smaller institutions to participate - for example by exploiting technical innovations - the better.
- The use of fine-tuning measures and an expensive "overdraft" (like today's German lombard loan) would vary to suit immediate needs.
- The final form of custody account usage would be for the collateralization of outstanding receivables from payment transactions. In Germany, these often represent the most important form of usage and are currently made up of around DM 200bn of available lombard facilities, a figure which is expected to increase (see Hartmann, 1994).

Because it is so important for the central bank to maintain its distance from the state, and thus to prevent a situation where the paper underpinning its operations are not concentrated too much on government stock, an arrangement could be considered under which lending facilities

[5] Szagunn, 1970, tends towards this conclusion; see also Geiger, 1982.

would be covered in full by private instruments, with no restrictions applying to other operations. The advantage of this would be that the generally more liquid and broadly based markets for government securities could be used for open market policy, something that is unimportant for the relatively sluggish standing facilities. The freedom to choose the type of collateral for payment transfers also appears to be justifiable because it is not an area which is sensitive to government influence.

3. Distribution of lending facilities not linked to transaction type

The volume of lending facilities would always have to be regulated to allow the central bank its control. This means that these facilities would either feature a preferential element (kept as low as possible) to allow institutions to maximize take-up (as in Germany and the Netherlands) or they would be auctioned. Irrespective of whether lending facilities are designed on a preferential or auction basis, the criterion for distributing them across the banks must be as fair as possible, i.e. it should not distort competition.

In this context, it would be worth considering the development of a method of calculating quotas not linked to any specific transaction types (wherever possible), and in particular to lending operations. From a theoretical perspective, a calculation based on capital would be justified because this is the key comparable figure for banks with different business orientations. This could also be considered for more pragmatic reasons, firstly because a revised arrangement must be agreed in Europe in any case, and secondly because capital adequacy regulations have already been harmonized in the Member States.

To avoid even the slightest hint of mistaken incentives, the capital required for stability reasons (whether it is the sole basis of calculation or in combination with others) should not be associated with any "coercion", and priority should be given to a solution involving a preferential interest rate. Establishing this as a discount rate fixed for long periods would only be effective if there was a sufficient gap between it and the market rate; in turn, this would exacerbates the problem of subsidies. This rate should therefore be linked to the repo rate for the same period and feature a minimum incentive of a few tenths of a percentage point.

The alternative to a quota-based distribution has been discribed in Chapter 3.5: in Dutch-style auctions, the banks' bids would be the repo rate of the identical maturity, plus/minus a certain margin. For the quota scheme as well as for the auction scheme, the maturity of this facility might be longer than for standard SRTs. This can be seen as an element of steadiness in monetary policy and it would support particularly small banks by reducing transaction costs.

This is not entirely satisfactory from a theoretical viewpoint because such an architecture fixes an inverted or flat interest rate structure for central bank credit. Compared with the present situation in Germany, however, it is still an improvement because the interest rate gap which affects the subsidy component can be smaller than it is for the discount rate. In particular, it would eliminate any temporary restraint in taking up rediscount credits due to expectations of a cut in interest rates.

4. Link minimum reserves and working balances

With minimum reserves performing a purely technical function, there is no longer any inherent link to refinancing and thus no convincing justification for a similar method of calculation (as is currently the case in Germany or the Netherlands, for example). On the one hand, the technical function is designed to cushion demand for central bank money. On the other, the minimum reserves must be higher than the working balances to be effective. Because the level of working balances may be closely linked to the volume of payments of individual banks and not merely their (short-term) deposits, it would be logical to examine the calculation method for minimum reserves to establish whether there are any meaningful indicators.

At a more detailed level, this study of possible orientation towards the payments system may identify - amongst other things - the problem that each bank's working balance may not rise with the volume of its payment transactions (due to the effects of scale or the structural effects of payment system networks). The extent to which a balanced volume of payments represents a stable basis of calculation should also be investigated, because the volume of payments in Germany is currently running at around fifty times the level of minimum reserves (see Remsperger, 1994). This involves empirical questions which cannot be answered on the basis of published data. In this respect, it is a theoretically motivated proposal requiring empirical verification.

As regards the actual level of the reserve requirement ratios, a comparison of the relevant countries shows that despite its tremendous adjustment efforts, Germany is still conspicuous by its unusually high ratios. This is the case not only on a European basis, but also in comparison with the USA, which also has a decentralized banking system. It seems quite clear that the most recent cuts in US reserve requirement ratios did not result in any unacceptable deterioration in money market management in terms of interest rate volatility (see Brunner/Lown, 1993).

Finally, it has also been argued that on the one hand, non-interest-bearing minimum reserves should not result in any distortion of competition, but on the other that working balances represent the cost of payments, which should not be subsidized. The upshot of this train of thought is a situation where interest should only be paid on the volume of reserves exceeding the working balances. However, this implies that the ratio of working balances to minimum reserves - or to put it another way, the proportion of involuntary reserves - will not vary too much between the institutions. The extent to which problems could arise in practice, and how these could be overcome, would have to be examined empirically.

5. The repo rate as the only key interest rate

If interest on involuntary reserves and overdraft interest were to be linked to the repo rate in the same way as the rate for lending facilities, there would effectively be only a single central bank interest rate (see Jarchow, 1995, p. 435, to this effect). This would be most desirable in terms of the impact of central bank policy and would even be superior to outright concentration on open market operations, because it would change not only the marginal interest rate, but also the rate for holdings.

4.4 Implementation of the concepts in Europe

A concept should not merely be well thought-out at a theoretical level, it should also stand a good chance of being implemented to avoid being ineffective. What are the factors which will determine whether a concept is capable of being implemented in Europe? These are likely to be the following four aspects:

- Instruments can be implemented most easily if they are already in place in the participating countries.
- It would probably be advantageous if they can be based not only on tradition, but also on theoretical and political principles.
- Instruments favoured by the Bundesbank are likely to have a slight edge, because it is the negotiation partner with the most weight.
- Finally, there must be a compromise for two reasons. In negotiations between parties which are essentially equals, it is standard practice for

all sides to make some concessions. Secondly, such a compromise distributes the cost of adjustment across all countries.

If the three concepts are compared against these four aspects, specific advantages and disadvantages become apparent. For pragmatic reasons, it appears justified to ignore the countries of Southern Europe on the grounds already discussed, and to restrict the discussion to the three key instruments.

The lean concept can probably count on support above all from the United Kingdom, as it largely corresponds to the British philosophy and institutions. For the same reason, it may well gain some support in France, which also operates with market makers, has a relatively low minimum reserve requirement, and so on. In contrast, the conservative concept has no comparable support, because even the Bundesbank disassociates itself from it. Within the Bundesbank it is most likely to be the Land Central Banks which will tend to favour this concept, as it strengthens their role to a greater extent than the lean concept. However, this interest-driven position could apply to at least the same extent to the decentralized concept. Jochimsen writes (1994b, p. 5): "As a bank of issue, however, we have always attached great importance to achieving the greatest degree of direct sales of our product 'central bank money'". The decentralized concept may also count on a sympathetic hearing in the Netherlands. Moreover, it can rely on its ties with the principle of subsidiarity; although its implementation may mean little to the representatives of centralized financial systems, it may accommodate the interests of smaller entities, such as small banks and countries or the non-centralized entities at central banks, for example the German Land Central Banks.

There is some conflict about the instruments of minimum reserves and refinancing policy. There may be a chance of compromise on minimum reserves by reducing them to an absolute minimum, for example by restricting them to the function of a liquidity cushion, and by making them interest-bearing (at least in part). Such a position could probably be acceptable in Germany, France and the Netherlands, where the instrument already exists. As their most determined champion, the Bundesbank's argument is really based only on their use as a liquidity cushion. The Netherlands pay interest on them and France has heavily cut the reserve requirement ratio. In Germany and France, they are elastic across a compliance period; this is desired in the Netherlands, but is actually undertaken using standing facilities.

Finally, refinancing policy is the most critical of all the instruments. If it is designed as extensively as suggested above for lending facilities in terms of the paper used, then there are unlikely to be serious objections to this instrument based on economic theory. It would accommodate the institutional situation in France, and it would mean an acceptable, perhaps even overdue reform in Germany. The major point of criticism would then be directed at the sacrifice of flexibility compared with open market policy, and a minor degree of distortion of competition due to the quotas, if the latter were to be retained. Both of these seem justifiable if "real world situations" are compared. This would see the ECB retaining a tremendous degree of flexibility, in concrete terms to at least the same extent as the Bundesbank today, but with probably lower requirements. Competitive distortions would be practically eliminated by the flexible ratio for standing facilities (and possibly changes to the method of calculation), and should be weighed against the politically undesirable lack of direct access by smaller institutions to central bank money which would ensue if there was a concentration on open market policy.

The objections against the core of the refinancing policy, the lending facilities, could probably be further reduced if this instrument were to be arranged in the form of a second line of open market policy. A concrete proposal was discussed which continues easy and direct access for small banks and - at the same time - avoids the use of non-market elements, such as quotas and subsides. At least from a Geman viewpoint, this line of thought seems to inhibit a reasonable degree of consensus as proponents of different concepts move into this direction: Issing (1996, p. 19) explicitly mentions the possibility of introducing a second tender model besides the standard SRTs. This second tender should be of longer maturity and exclusively based on private (in contrast to public) paper. The volume tender model for auctioning lending facilities, discussed by Hesse/Braasch (1996), was mentioned above. Proponents of a lean, a conservative and a decentralized concept are now proposing modifications to their original concept which are therefore converging to some degree.

Reviewing these aspects, it becomes clear that neither the lean nor the conservative concept can be realistically implemented in full. To a certain extent - in particular in view of its negligible minimum reserves - the decentralized concept is itself a "compromise" between the two other concepts. It will probably be easier to implement if standing facilities are kept as lean as possible and do not interfere with fair competition.

5 Result of the study

The result of this analysis is a proposal for the design of the monetary policy instruments of the European Central Bank. This has been termed a decentralized concept. The outline of the derivation of this concept is as follows:

The first chapter restricted the study to the three key instruments of open market, minimum reserve and refinancing policy. The three goals of efficiency, fair competition and decentralization were also elaborated.

The contents of this framework were then added gradually in Chapter Two. The status quo of the ECB prohibits any fiscal component of central bank money creation; international monetary policy trends point towards the relative rise of open market policy and a lesser role for the other instruments; and an analysis of national role-models in the EU highlighted the often contrary positions of Germany and the United Kingdom. One interim result was that minimum reserves and refinancing policy in particular are contentious. The consensus on these two instruments does not go beyond the acceptance of a minimum reserve requirement and the function of refinancing policy as a safety valve for temporary demand for central bank money.

For this reason, Chapter Three concentrated on a more detailed analysis of these two instruments against the background of the three goals of the study. The examination of efficiency aspects showed that minimum reserves can only be justified to a very limited extent, and a refinancing policy - at least in the form practised in Germany - not at all. Although there are some convincing arguments in favour, such as the function of shielding the real economy, there are other monetary policy instruments than those discussed here which could tackle the root of the problem more adequately.

The analysis in terms of competition policy also showed that open market policy is clearly the instrument of choice as long as the system of minimum reserves and rediscount quotas follows the German example. However, competitive distortions can be considerably reduced if there are substantial reforms to this system. Market-oriented conditions are also fundamental because price distortion is the greatest problem associated with this instrument.

The analysis of the instruments in terms of their impact on decentralization produced the following picture: in the first stage, indicators of decentralization were proposed and potential conflicts with the goal of efficiency - including beyond the area of monetary policy management - were examined. The results showed that there appear to be no problems with the politically desirable concept of decentralization. The ranking of the three instruments derived in the second stage produced a different pattern: open market policy was now seen to be problematic. In contrast, a more liberal refinancing policy in the form of standing facilities appeared to be advantageous and minimum reserves - in the form of a liquidity cushion - were probably beneficial. Due to the uniformity of monetary policy, however, there was likely to be no relevant scope for decision-making powers at a subsidiary level in terms of the decentralized implementation of monetary policy.

These considerations show that although an economic analysis can reduce the number of options, it cannot provide an unquestionably "optimum" solution for the instruments of monetary policy. It is rather the case that fundamental assumptions about the functioning of the financial system and the consequent tasks of monetary policy determine the combination and design of those instruments regarded as feasible. In simple terms, three concepts can be derived: a "lean", a "conservative" and a "decentralized" concept. By backing the assumptions and accepting the implications, each of these concepts, all of which are geared to achieving monetary stability, can be justified even in its purely theoretical form.

To ensure that monetary policy also takes account of the goal of subsidiarity, priority was given to the decentralized concept. This is not designed either to actively promote or to obstruct decentralization, but merely to facilitate it effectively. Using the three goals as a benchmark, short-term management efficiency would still be ensured by the considerable use of open market operations. In contrast, decentralization essentially makes it easier to use standing facilities to the greatest possible extent, without these restricting the flexibility vital to monetary policy. In their purely technical function as a liquidity cushion, minimum reserves also facilitate decentralization. To ensure that the problem instruments do not distort competition, a wider range of eligible paper, near-market interest rates and different methods of calculation were proposed. Finally, cost efficiency would be substantially enhanced by harmonizing the basic technical components of refinancing and open market policy.

From this perspective, the array of instruments proposed is comparatively lean because they are simple to operate. The multi-instrument approach and the stronger weighting given to private-sector securities correspond to the conservative concept. Due to the inclusion of these elements of other concepts, it may not be particularly difficult to achieve agreement on its implementation, as long as such an agreement would involve only Germany, France and the Netherlands, for example, as was mentioned above for minimum reserves. Germany and the Netherlands are already familiar with the instrument of standing facilities, albeit with distinctive, country-specific features. In contrast, France could contribute the broad definition of eligible paper.

To sum up, the decentralized concept of monetary policy instruments for Europe elaborated here could therefore provide an acceptable basis of discussion. This concept allows the efficient management of monetary policy and ensures the greatest possible degree of fair competition (thus probably making it superior to the current German instruments). In contrast to the other competing concepts, it is not designed to relinquish decentralization to existing structures, but rather to deliberately adjust these to ensure that decentralization is made easier.

References

Baltensperger, Ernst (1982), Reserve Requirements and Economic Stability, in: Journal of Money, Credit, and Banking, Vol.14, No.2, pp.205-215.

Baltensperger, Ernst (1982a), Reserve Requirements and Optimal Money Balances, in: Zeitschrift für Wirtschafts- und Sozialwissenschaften, Vol.102, No.3, pp.225-236.

Baltensperger, Ernst (1994), Commentary to Hesse/Braasch, in: Bernhard Gahlen/Helmut Hesse/Hans Jürgen Ramser (eds.), Europäische Integrationsprobleme aus wirtschaftswissenschaftlicher Sicht, Schriftenreihe des Wirtschaftswissenschaftlichen Seminars Ottobeuren, Vol.23, Tübingen: J.C.B. Mohr (Paul Siebeck), pp.185-188.

Bank of England (1988), Bank of England Operations in the Sterling Money Market, in: Bank of England Quarterly Bulletin, August, pp.391-409.

Banque de France (1992), The Banque de France - History, Organization, Role, Paris.

Banque de France (1993), Annual Report 1992, Paris.

Beckh, Susanne (1986), Die Wertpapierpensionsgeschäfte der Bundesbank, in: Sparkasse, Vol.103, No.11, pp.484-487.

Benston, George J. (1994), Universal Banking, in: Journal of Economic Perspectives, Vol.8, No.3, pp.121-143.

Berger, Allen H./William C. Hunter/Stephen G. Timme (1993), The Efficiency of Financial Institutions: A Review and Preview of Research Past, Present, and Future, in: Journal of Banking and Finance, Vol.17, pp.221-249.

Bernanke, Ben S./Alan S. Blinder (1992), The Federal Funds Rate and the Channels of Monetary Transmission, in: American Economic Review, Vol.82, No.4, pp.901-921.

Bernanke, Ben/Frederic Mishkin (1993), Central Bank Behavior and the Strategy of Monetary Policy: Observations from Six Industrialized Countries, in: NBER Macroeconomics Annual, Vol.7, pp.183-228.

Bisignano, Joseph (1996), Varieties of Monetary Policy Operating Procedures: Balancing Monetary Objectives with Market Efficiency, Bank for International Settlements, Working Paper No.35, Basle.

Bockelmann, Horst (1996), Unterschiede in den nationalen Finanzstrukturen und ihre makroökonomische Bedeutung, in: Dieter Duwendag (ed.), Finanzmärkte, Finanzinnovationen und Geldpolitik; Schriften des Vereins für Socialpolitik N.F., Vol.242, Berlin: Duncker & Humblot, pp.11-39.

Bofinger, Peter (1996), Mindestreserve und Feinsteuerung des Geldmarktzinses, in: Peter Bofinger/Karl-Heinz Ketterer (eds.), Neuere Entwicklungen in der Geldtheorie und Geldpolitik, Festschrift für Norbert Kloten, Tübingen: J.C.B. Mohr (Paul Siebeck), pp.295-324.

Borchert, Manfred (1986), Mindestreservekonzeptionen, Wiesbaden: Gabler.

Boyd, John H./David E. Runkle (1993), Size and Performance of Banking Firms, Testing the Predictions of Theory, in: Journal of Monetary Economics, Vol.31, pp.47-67.

Braasch, Bernd/Helmut Hesse (1994), Innovationen im Zahlungsverkehr und ihre Auswirkungen auf die Geldpolitik, in: Manfred Bodin/ Lothar Hübl (eds.), Banken in gesamtwirtschaftlicher Verantwortung, Zum 65. Geburtstag von Dr. Gebhard Dirksen, Stuttgart: Deutscher Sparkassenverlag, pp.40-63.

Breig, Hildegard (1996), Financial Regulation and the Banks' Role in European Economies, in: Richard Tilly/Paul J.J. Welfens (eds.), European Economic Integration as a Challenge to Industry and Government, Berlin et al.: Springer, pp.325-347.

Brimmer, Andrew (1989), Central Banking and Systemic Risks in Capital Markets, in: Journal of Economic Perspectives, Vol.3, No.2, pp.3-16.

Brunner, Allan D./Cara S. Lown (1993), The Effects of Lower Reserve Requirements on Money Market Volatility, in: American Economic Review, Vol.83, No.2, pp.199-205.

Carstensen, Meinhard (1988), Gedanken zur Mindestreservepolitik aus der Sicht der Geschäftsbanken, in: Ehrlicher/Simmert (1988), pp.93-108.

Chick, Victoria (1988), The Evolution of the Banking System and the Theory of Monetary Policy, in: Wolfgang Gebauer (ed.), Geld-Währung-Kapitalmarkt Working Papers, No.8, Frankfurt/M.

Cothren, Richard (1987), Asymmetric Information and Optimal Bank Reserves, in: Journal of Money, Credit, and Banking, Vol.19, No.1, pp.68-77.

Cothren, Richard D./ R.N. Waud (1994), On the Optimality of Reserve Requirements, in: Journal of Money, Credit, and Banking, Vol.26, No.4, pp.827-838.

Cottarelli, Carlo/Giovanni Ferri/Andrea Generale (1995), Bank Lending Rates and Financial Structure in Italy, in: IMF Staff Papers, Vol.42, No.3, pp.670-700.

Cottarelli, Carlo/Angeliki Kourelis (1994), Financial Structure, Bank Lending Rates, and the Transmission Mechanism of Monetary Policy, in: IMF Staff Papers, Vol.41, No.4, pp.587-623.

Crockett, Andrew (1994), Financial Innovation: Macro-Economic and Micro-Prudential Consequences, Paper presented at the 25th Konstanz Seminar on Monetary Theory and Monetary Policy, 26.5.1994.

Cukierman, Alex (1995), How Can the European Central Bank Become Credible?, Paper presented at the CEPR/Irving Fisher Society-Conference "What Monetary Policy for the European Central Bank?", Frankfurt/M.

De Grauwe, Paul (1996), The Economics of Convergence Towards Monetary Union in Europe, in: Weltwirtschaftliches Archiv, Vol.132, No.1, pp.1-27.

Deutsche Bundesbank (1975), Regelungen für die Bemessung von Rediskont-Kontingenten, in: Monthly Reports, Vol.27, No.4, pp.21ff.

Deutsche Bundesbank (1983), The Bundesbank's Transactions in Securities under Repurchase Agreements, in: Monthly Reports, Vol.35, No.5, pp.23ff.

Deutsche Bundesbank (1985), Recent Developments with Respect to the Bundesbank's Repurchase Agreements, in: Monthly Reports, Vol.37, No.10, pp.18ff.

Deutsche Bundesbank (1990), Minimum Reserve Arrangements Abroad, in: Monthly Reports, Vol.42, No.3, pp.21ff.

Deutsche Bundesbank (1993), Annual Report for the Year 1992, Frankfurt/M.

Deutsche Bundesbank (1993a), Off-Balance-Sheet Activities of German Banks, in: Monthly Reports, Vol.45, No.10, pp.45ff.

Deutsche Bundesbank (1994), The Second Stage of European Economic and Monetary Union, in: Monthly Reports, Vol.46, No.1, pp.23ff.

Deutsche Bundesbank (1994a), Money Market Management by the Deutsche Bundesbank, in: Monthly Reports, Vol.46, No.5, pp.61-75.

Deutsche Bundesbank (1995), The Monetary Policy of the Deutsche Bundesbank, Frankfurt/M.

Deutsche Bundesbank (1995a), Review of the Monetary Target and Restucturing of the Minimum Reserve Regulations, in: Monthly Reports, Vol.47, No.7, pp.17ff.

Deutsche Bundesbank (1996), Finanzmarktvolatilität und ihre Auswirkungen auf die Geldpolitik, in: Monthly Reports, Vol.48, No.4, pp.53-70.

Edwards, Jeremy/Klaus Fischer (1994), Banks, Finance, and Investment in Germany, Cambridge: Cambridge University Press.

Ehrlicher, Werner (1973), Zur Neuordnung des Instrumentariums der Deutschen Bundesbank, in: Kredit und Kapital, Vol.6, No.2, pp.111-133.

Ehrlicher, Werner (1981), Geldtheorie und Geldpolitik VI: Geldpolitik, in: Handwörterbuch der Wirtschaftswissenschaften, Vol.3, Stuttgart et al., pp.423-451.

Ehrlicher, Werner (1989), Geldkapitalbildung und Realkapitalbildung von 1950 bis 1987, in: Norbert Bub/Dieter Duwendag/Rudolf Richter (eds.), Geldwertsicherung und Wirtschaftsstabilität, Festschrift für Helmut Schlesinger zum 65. Geburtstag, Frankfurt/M., pp.27-55.

Ehrlicher, Werner/Hans-Hermann Francke (1988), Zum Phänomen überproportionaler Geldvermögensbildung im Finanzierungssystem der Bundesrepublik Deutschland, in: Bernd Rudoph/Jochen Wilhelm (eds.), Bankpolitik, finanzielle Unternehmensführung und die Theorie der Finanzmärkte, Festschrift für Hans-Jacob Krümmel zur Vollendung des 60. Lebensjahres, Berlin: Duncker & Humblot, pp.393-407.

Ehrlicher, Werner/Diethart B. Simmert (1988) (eds.), Wandlungen des geldpolitischen Instrumentariums der Deutschen Bundesbank, Supplements to Kredit und Kapital, Vol.10, Berlin: Duncker & Humblot.

Eichengreen, Barry (1993), European Monetary Unification, in: Journal of Economic Literature, Vol.31, No.3, pp.1321-1357.

European Monetary Institute (1995), Annual Report 1994, Frankfurt/M.

European Monetary Institute (1996), Annual Report 1995, Frankfurt/M.

Fama, Eugene F. (1991), Efficient Capital Markets: II, in: Journal of Finance, Vol.46, No.5, pp.1575-1617.

Feinman, Joshua N. (1993), Reserve Requirements: History, Current Practice, and Potential Reforms, in: Federal Reserve Bulletin, Vol.79, No.6, pp.569-589.

Feldsieper, Manfred/Paul Terres (1994), Die Entwicklung des geldpolitischen Instrumentariums der Deutschen Bundesbank, in: WISU, Vol.23, No.6, pp.536-544.

Francke, Hans-Hermann (1995), Commentary to Tietmeyer (1995), in: Lüder Gerken (ed.), Europa zwischen Ordnungswettbewerb und Harmonisierung - Europäische Ordnungspolitik im Zeichen der Subsidiarität, Berlin et al.: Springer, pp.149-152.

Frankel, Allen B./John D. Montgomery (1991), Financial Structure: An International Perspective, in: Brookings Papers on Economic Activity, No.1, pp.257-310.

Frankel, Jeffrey A. (1992), Measuring International Capital Mobility: A Review, in: American Economic Review, Vol.82, No.2, pp.197-202.

Friedman, Milton (1953), The Case for Flexible Exchange Rates, in: the same, Essays in Positive Economics, Chicago: Chicago University Press, pp.157-203.

Friedman, Milton (1960), A Program for Monetary Stability, New York: Fordham University Press.

Friedmann, Willy (1988), Die Mindestreserve im deutschen Finanzsystem, in: Ehrlicher/Simmert (1988), pp.79-91.

Gaddum, Johann Wilhelm (1994), Ziele und Möglichkeiten deutscher Geldpolitik in Europa, in: Wirtschaftsdienst, Vol.74, No.2, pp.72-77.

Gaddum, Johann Wilhelm (1994a), Aktuelle Fragen der Geldpolitik, in: Deutsche Bundesbank, Auszüge aus Presseartikeln, No.32, 9.5.1994.

Geiger, Helmut (1982), Instrumentelle Aspekte der Geldpolitik, in: Werner Ehrlicher/Diethart B. Simmert (eds.) (1982), Geld- und Währungspolitik in der Bundesrepublik Deutschland, Supplements to Kredit und Kapital, Vol.7, Berlin: Duncker & Humblot, pp.195-205.

Geiger, Helmut (1988), Das Verhältnis von Refinanzierungs- und Offenmarktpolitik, in: Ehrlicher/Simmert (1988), pp.129-142.

Gerlach, Stefan/Frank Smets (1995), The Monetary Transmission Mechanism: Evidence from the G-7 Countries, CEPR Discussion Paper No.1219, London.

Gischer, Horst (1994), Wirkungsaussichten von Diskontpolitik im Geldmengenkonzept, in: Christian Hipp et al. (eds.), Geld, Finanzwirtschaft, Banken und Versicherungen, Karlsruhe, pp.173-192.

Gischer, Horst (1996), Zinsen, Investitionstätigkeit und Verschuldung - Konsequenzen der Geldpolitik für den Unternehmenssektor, Working Paper, University of Dortmund.

Glaum, Martin (1994), Informationseffizienz der Devisenmärkte und unternehmerisches Wechselkurs-Risikomanagement, in: Kredit und Kapital, Vol.27, No.1, pp.67-99.

Goldstein, Morris et al. (1993), International Capital Markets Part I, Exchange Rate Management and International Capital Flows, IMF, World Economic Outlook and Financial Surveys, Washington D.C.

Goodhart, Charles (1988), Why Do Banks Need a Centralbank?, in: Oxford Economic Papers, Vol.39, pp.75-89.

Goodhart, Charles (1992), The Objectives for, and Conduct of, Monetary Policy in the 1990s, LSE Financial Markets Group, Special Paper No.49, London.

Goodhart, Charles (1995), Financial Globalisation, Derivatives, Volatility and the Challenge for the Policies of Central Banks, LSE Financial Markets Group, Special Paper No.74, London.

Goodhart, Charles (1996), Why Do Monetary Authorities Smooth Interest Rates?, LSE Financial Markets Group, Special Paper No.81, London.

Goodhart, Charles/Jose Viñals (1994), Strategy and Tactics of Monetary Policy: Examples from Europe and the Antipodes, in: J. Fuhrer (ed.), Goals, Guidelines and Constraints Facing Monetary Policymakers, Federal Reserve Bank of Boston, Conference Series, No.38, pp.139-187.

Gordon, David B./Eric M. Leeper (1994), The Dynamic Impacts of Monetary Policy: An Exercise in Tentative Identification, in: Journal of Political Economy, Vol.102, No.6, pp.1228-1247.

Greenbaum, Stuart I./Anjan V. Thakor (1989), Bank Reserve Requirements as an Impediment to Signaling, in: Economic Inquiry, Vol.27, No.1, pp.75-91.

Guesnerie, Roger/Jean-Charles Rochet (1993), (De)Stabilizing Speculation on Futures Markets, An Alternative View Point, in: European Economic Review, Vol.37, pp.1043-1063.

Häusler, Gerd (1994), The Competitive Position of Germany as a Financial Centre as Seen by a Central Banker, in: Deutsche Bundesbank, Auszüge aus Presseartikeln, No.36, 25.5.1994.

Hagen, Jürgen von (1987), Money Stock Targeting with Alternative Reserve Requirement Systems, in: Zeitschrift für Wirtschafts- und Sozialwissenschaften, Vol.107, No.3, pp.379-395.

Hartmann, Wendelin (1994), Geldpolitik und Zahlungsverkehr, in: Deutsche Bundesbank, Auszüge aus Presseartikeln, No.18, 16.3.1994.

Hasche-Preuße, Christine (1994), Möglichkeiten zur Förderung des deutschen Geldmarktes im internationalen Wettbewerb, in: Kredit und Kapital, Vol.27, No.1, pp.135-153.

Hesse, Helmut (1991), Gebieten internationale Gründe die Abschaffung der Mindestreserve?, in: Weltwirtschaftliches Archiv, Vol.127, No.3, pp.429-451.

Hesse, Helmut (1994), Als Wissenschaftler in der Politik?, in: Deutsche Bundesbank, Auszüge aus Preseartikeln, No.47, 5.7.1994, pp.6-15.

Hesse, Helmut/Bernd Braasch (1994), Zum "optimalen" Instrumentarium der Europäischen Zentralbank, in: Bernhard Gahlen/Helmut Hesse/Hans Jürgen Ramser (eds.), Europäische Integrationsprobleme aus wirtschaftswissenschaftlicher Sicht, Schriftenreihe des Wirtschaftswissenschaftlichen Seminars Ottobeuren, Vol.23, Tübingen: J.C.B. Mohr (Paul Siebeck), pp.161-184.

Hesse, Helmut/Bernd Braasch (1996), "Standing facilities" - als geldpolitisches Instrument einer europäischen Notenbank verzichtbar?, in: Peter Bofinger/Karl-Heinz Ketterer (eds.), Neuere Entwicklungen in der Geldtheorie und Geldpolitik, Festschrift für Norbert Kloten, Tübingen: J.C.B. Mohr, pp.275-293.

Holland, Robert C. (1970), The Federal Discount Mechanism as an Instrument for Dealing with Banking Market Imperfections, in: Journal of Money, Credit, and Banking, Vol.2, May, pp.138-146.

Horrigan, Brian R. (1988), Are Reserve Requirements Relevant for Economic Stabilization?, in: Journal of Monetary Economics, Vol.21, January, pp.97-105.

Icard, André (1994), Experience Gained with Monetary Policy Instruments in France, in: Deutsche Bundesbank, Auszüge aus Presseartikeln, No.41, 13.6.1994, pp.2-6.

Issing, Otmar (1988), Das geldpolitische Instrumentarium unter dem Aspekt der Wettbewerbsneutralität, in: Ehrlicher/Simmert (1988), pp.219-240.

Issing, Otmar (1988a), Das Instrumentarium der Deutschen Bundesbank - Argumente für eine Neuorientierung, in: Gottfried Bombach/ Bernhard Gahlen/Alfred E. Ott (eds.), Geldtheorie und Geldpolitik, Schriftenreihe des Wirtschaftswissenschaftlichen Seminars Ottobeuren, Vol.17, Tübingen: J.C.B. Mohr (Paul Siebeck), pp.61-75.

Issing, Otmar (1993), Einführung in die Geldpolitik, München: Vahlen, 5.ed.

Issing, Otmar (1994), Experience Gained with Monetary Policy Instruments in Germany, in: Deutsche Bundesbank, Auszüge aus Presseartikeln, No.41, 13.6.1994, pp.22-28.

Issing, Otmar (1994a), Notenbank und Börse - Geldpolitik und der Finanzplatz Deutschland, in: Deutsche Bundesbank, Auszüge aus Presseartikeln, No.47, 5.7.1994, pp.2-6.

Issing, Otmar (1996), Bedingungen für stabiles Geld in Deutschland und Europa, in: Deutsche Bundesbank, Auszüge aus Presseartikeln, No.6, 31.1.1996, pp.16-22.

Issing, Otmar/Karlheinz Bischofberger (1996), Derivate und Geldpolitik, in: Duwendag, Dieter (ed.), Finanzmärkte, Finanzinnovationen und Geldpolitik, Schriften des Vereins für Socialpolitik, N.F., Vol.242, Berlin: Duncker & Humblot, pp.111-137.

Issing, Otmar/Bernd Rudolph (1988), Der Rediskontkredit - Die geldpolitische Bedeutung und der Einfluß des Rediskontkredits der Deutschen Bundesbank auf die Wettbewerbssituation im Bankensektor, Stuttgart: Deutscher Sparkassenverlag.

Jarchow, Hans-Joachim (1995), Zur Strategie und zum Instrumentarium der Europäischen Zentralbank, in: Aussenwirtschaft, Vol.50, No.3, pp.423-442.

Jerger, Jürgen/Lukas Menkhoff (1995), Refinancing Policy Options of the European Central Bank, in: Hans-Hermann Francke/Eberhart Ketzel (eds.), Europäische Währungsunion - Von der Konzeption zur Gestaltung, Supplements to Kredit und Kapital, Vol.14, Berlin: Duncker & Humblot, forthcoming.

Jochimsen, Reimut (1993), Perspektiven des Finanzplatzes Deutschland in den 90er Jahren, in: Deutsche Bundesbank, Auszüge aus Presseartikeln, No.88, 10.12.1993, pp.2-9.

Jochimsen, Reimut (1994), Perspektiven der europäischen Wirtschafts- und Währungsunion, Köln: Bund-Verlag.

Jochimsen, Reimut (1994a), Ausführungen anläßlich der Veranstaltung des Freundeskreises der Geldhändler in Nordrhein-Westfalen, in: Deutsche Bundesbank, Auszüge aus Presseartikeln, No.16, 8.3.1994.

Kasman, Bruce (1992), A Comparison of Monetary Policy Operating Procedures in Six Industrial Countries, in: Federal Reserve Bank of New York Quarterly Review, Vol.17, No.2, pp.5-24.

Kath, Dietmar (1993), Mindestreserven in Europa, in: Österreichische Sparkassenzeitung, Vol.80, No.14, pp.322-326.

King, Mervyn (1993), The Bundesbank: A View from the Bank of England, Bank of England Quarterly Bulletin, May 1993, pp.269-273.

King, Mervyn (1994), Monetary Policy Instruments: The UK Experience, in: Deutsche Bundesbank, Auszüge aus Presseartikeln, No.41, 13.6.1994, pp.16-21.

King, Robert G./Ross Levine (1993), Finance and Growth: Schumpeter Might Be Right, in: Quarterly Journal of Economics, Vol.108, No.3, pp.717-737.

Kirchgässner, Gebhard (1993), Vom Nutzen der Wirtschaftstheorie für die Wirtschaftspolitik, in: Konjunkturpolitik, Vol.39, No.4, pp.201-225.

Kneeshaw, J.T. (1995), A Survey of Non-Financial Sector Balance Sheets in Industrialised Countries: Implications for the Monetary Policy Transmission Mechanism, BIS Working Paper No.25, Basle.

Kneeshaw, J.T./P. Van den Bergh (1989), Changes in Central Bank Money Market Operating Procedures in the 1980s, BIS Economic Papers No.23, Basle.

Koebnick, Hans-Jürgen (1994), Nationale Zentralbanken sollen mit dem Rating betraut werden, in: Handelsblatt, 8.6.1994.

König, Reiner (1994), Geld- und Währungspolitik zu Beginn der zweiten Stufe der EWWU, in: Wolfgang Gebauer (ed.), Geld-Währung-Kapitalmarkt Working Papers, No.32, Frankfurt/M.

Krupp, Hans-Jürgen (1996), Zur Entwicklung geldpolitischer Instrumente im Europäischen Währungssystem unter Berücksichtigung der kleineren Geschäftsbanken, in: Deutsche Bundesbank, Auszüge aus Presseartikeln, No.33, 24.5.1996, pp.8-12.

LCB (Land Central Bank, Landeszentralbank in der Freien Hansestadt Bremen, in Niedersachsen und Sachsen-Anhalt) (1996), Volatilität von Wechselkursen und Zinsen, Offprint from the Annual Report for the Year 1995, pp.1-36.

Lehment, Harmen/Joachim Scheide (1992), Die Europäische Wirtschafts- und Währungsunion: Probleme des Übergangs, in: Die Weltwirtschaft, No.1, pp.50-67.

Lombra, Raymond E./Raymond G. Torto (1977), Discount Rate and Announcement Effects, in: Quarterly Journal of Economics, Vol.91, No.1, pp.171-176.

Loungani, Prakash/Mark Rush (1995), The Effect of Changes in Reserve Requirements on Investment and GNP, in: Journal of Money, Credit, and Banking, Vol.27, No.2, pp.511-526.

Mayer, Colin/Xavier Vives (1993), Introduction, in: the same (eds.), Capital Markets and Financial Intermediation, Cambridge: Cambridge University Press, pp.1-11.

Meister, Edgar (1994), Risiken in derivativen Finanzinstrumenten und Möglichkeiten der Begrenzung, in: Deutsche Bundesbank, Auszüge aus Presseartikeln, No.21, 30.3.1994.

Meister, Edgar/Gerhard Hofmann (1994), Mindestreserve fit gemacht für Europa, in: Zeitschrift für das gesamte Kreditwesen, Vol.47, No.5, pp.210-214.

Menkhoff, Lukas (1995), Spekulative Verhaltensweisen auf Devisenmärkten, Tübingen: J.C.B. Mohr (Paul Siebeck).

Menkhoff, Lukas (1995a), Refinanzierungs- oder Offenmarktpolitik für Europa?, in: Wirtschaftsdienst, Vol.75, No.6, pp.313-319.

Menkhoff, Lukas (1996), Geldpolitische Instrumente der Europäischen Zentralbank, Eine Analyse unter den Aspekten Effizienz, Wettbewerbsneutralität und Dezentralität; Wissenschaft für die Praxis: Abt. Forschung, Vol.5, Stuttgart: Deutscher Sparkassenverlag, 2.ed.

Menkhoff, Lukas (1996a), Competitive Neutrality of Monetary Policy Instruments for EMU, in: Paul J.J. Welfens (ed.), European Monetary Union: Transition, International Impacts, and Policy Options, forthcoming.

Menkhoff, Lukas (1996b), Institutsgröße, Offenmarktpolitik und Wettbewerbsneutralität: Ergebnisse einer Befragung von Sparkassen, Working Paper, Aachen University of Technology.

Menkhoff, Lukas/Jochen Michaelis (1995), Ist die Tobin-Steuer tatsächlich "tot"?, in: Jahrbuch für Wirtschaftswissenschaften, Vol.46, No.1, pp.34-54.

Menkhoff, Lukas/Friedrich L. Sell (1992), Überlegungen zu einem optimalen DM-Währungsraum, in: Zeitschrift für Wirtschafts- und Sozialwissenschaften, Vol.112, No.3, pp.379-400.

Meulendyke, Ann-Marie (1992), Reserve Requirements and the Discount Window in Recent Decades, in: Federal Reserve Bank of New York Quarterly Review, Vol.17, No.3, pp.25-43.

Meyer-Horn, Klaus (1993), Mindestreserven nur noch Ultima ratio?, in: Sparkasse, Vol.110, No.4, pp.153-158.

Meyer-Horn, Klaus (1993a), Entwurf für eine Initiativ-Stellungnahme zur "Mindestreservepolitik im Binnenmarkt", vorgelegt für die Sitzung der Fachgruppe für Wirtschafts-, Finanz- und Währungsfragen am 9.3.1993.

Mishkin, Frederic S. (1993), Preventing Financial Crises: An International Perspective, Presented at the ESRI Banking Research Centre Conference "Interest Rate Movements: Causes and Effects", Dublin.

Monticelli, C./J. Viñals (1993), European Monetary Policy in Stage Three: What Are the Issues?, CEPR Occasional Paper, No.12, London.

Müller, Andrea (1992), Die Mindestreserve: Ausgestaltung und Wandlungen eines Instruments der deutschen Zentralbank seit 1948, Berlin: Duncker & Humblot.

Nautz, Dieter (1995), Zur Feinsteuerung des Geldmarktes durch die Wertpapierpensionsgeschäfte der Bundesbank, in: Zeitschrift für Wirtschafts- und Sozialwissenschaften, Vol.115, No.4, pp.623-644.

Neumann, Manfred J.M./Jürgen von Hagen (1995), The Strategy of Monetary Targeting: Can the German Experience Provide a Model for the ECB?, Paper presented at the CEPR/Irving Fisher Society-Conference "What Monetary Policy for the European Central Bank?", Frankfurt/M.

Pagano, Marco (1993), Financial Markets and Growth, An Overview, in: European Economic Review, Vol.37, pp.613-622.

Pagano, Marco/Ailsa Roell (1990), Stock Markets (incl. discussion), in: Economic Policy, Vol.5, No.1, pp.63-115.

Quintyn, Marc (1993), Managing Monetary Policy Reforms. Lessons from the French Experience, in: Banca Nazionale del Lavoro Quarterly Review, No.186, pp.275-298.

Reither, Franco (1985), Mindestreserven und gesamtwirtschaftliche Steuerung, in: Wirtschaftsdienst, Vol.65, No.10, pp.503-509.

Remolona, Eli M. (1992), The Recent Growth of Financial Derivative Markets, in: Federal Reserve Bank of New York Quarterly Review, Vol.17, No.4, pp.28-43.

Remsperger, Hermann (1994), Geldmarktpolitik aus Bankensicht, in: Die Bank, No.5, pp.260-265.

Remsperger, Hermann (1994a), Subsidiarität in der Zentralbankpolitik: Erfahrungen und Perspektiven, in: Wolfgang Filc/Claus Köhler (eds.), Integration oder Desintegration in der Weltwirtschaft?, Berlin: Duncker & Humblot, pp.13-35.

Remsperger, Hermann/Uwe Angenendt (1995), Freiwillige Reserven in der Europäischen Währungsunion, in: Die Bank, No.7, pp.401-406.

Rich, Georg (1995), Does the European Central Bank Need Minimum Reserves?, Paper presented at the CEPR/Irving Fisher Society-Conference "What Monetary Policy for the European Central Bank?", Frankfurt/M.

Richter, Rudolf (1991), Bankenregulierung aus der Sicht der neuen Institutionenökonomik, in: Jürgen Siebke (ed.), Finanzintermediation, Bankenregulierung und Finanzmarktintegration, Schriften des Vereins für Socialpolitik N.F., Vol.204, Berlin: Duncker & Humblot, pp.43-64.

Rohde, Armin/Diethard B. Simmert (1986), Mindestreserven: Ein überflüssiges Instrument der Geldpolitik, in: Wirtschaftsdienst, Vol.66, No.8, pp.404-410.

Schlesinger, Helmut (1987), Kapitalmarkt, Kapitalbildung und Kapitalallokation, in: Dieter Schneider (ed.), Kapitalmarkt und Finanzierung, Schriften des Vereins für Socialpolitik N.F., Vol.165, Berlin: Duncker & Humblot, pp.17-47.

Schlesinger, Helmut (1992), Grundfragen einer europäischen Zentralbankpolitik, in: Deutsche Bundesbank, Auszüge aus Presseartikeln, No.92, 21.12.1992.

Schmidt, Hartmut (1992), Die Rolle der Regionalbörsen am deutschen Kapitalmarkt heute und morgen (Part I), in: Kredit und Kapital, Vol.25, No.1, pp.110-134.

Schmidt, Hartmut (1992a), (Part II), in: Kredit und Kapital, Vol.25, No.2, pp.233-258.

Schmidt, Reinhard H. (1994),

Scholtens, L.J.R. (1992), Centralization in International Financial Intermediation: Theory, Practice, and Evidence for the European Community, in: Banca Nazionale del Lavoro Quarterly Review, No.182, pp.255-304.

Schulmann, Horst (1994), Europäische Zentralbank: Das Frankfurter Modell für die europäische Geldpolitik, in: Finanzplatz Frankfurt.

Sinn, Hans-Werner (1986), Risiko als Produktionsfaktor, in: Jahrbücher für Nationalökonomie und Statistik, Vol.201, No.6, pp.557-571.

Sprenkle, Case M. (1993), The Case of the Missing Currency, in: Journal of Economic Perspectives, Vol.7, No.4, pp.175-184.

Szagunn, Volkhard (1970), Bundesbankgeld durch Buchkredit? Gedanken zur Refinanzierung der Banken, in: Bank-Betrieb, No.10, pp.342-348.

Thomas, Karl (1988), Das Verhältnis von Refinanzierungs- und Offenmarktpolitik, in: Ehrlicher/Simmert (1988), pp.109-127.

Thomas, Karl (1990), Finanzmarktprobleme aus deutscher Sicht, in: Sparkasse, Vol.107, No.6, pp.251-258.

Tichy, Gunther (1990), Bankengröße und Effizienz, in: Kredit und Kapital, Vol.23, No.3, pp.358-389.

Tietmeyer, Hans (1994), Monetary Policy Instruments: National Experiences and European Perspectives, in: Deutsche Bundesbank, Auszüge aus Presseartikeln, No.41, 13.6.1994, pp.1-2.

Tietmeyer, Hans (1995) Auf dem Weg zur Währungsunion: Wo stehen wir?, in: Lüder Gerken (ed.), Europa zwischen Ordnungswettbewerb und Harmonisierung - Europäische Ordnungspolitik im Zeichen der Subsidiarität, Berlin et al.: Springer, pp.137-147.

Timmermann, Vincenz (1989), Finanzinnovationen und Globalisierung aus volkswirtschaftlicher Sicht, in: Jahrbuch für Sozialwissenschaft, Vol.40, pp.279-286.

Treutler, Hans-Jürgen (1992), Vorbereitung der einheitlichen Geldpolitik in der dritten Stufe der WWU, in: Wolfgang Gebauer (ed.), Geld-Währung-Kapitalmarkt Working Papers, No.27, Frankfurt/M.

Vanberg, Viktor (1992), Innovation, Cultural Evolution, and Economic Growth, in: Ulrich Witt (ed.), Explaining Process and Change, Approaches to Evolutionary Economics, Ann Arbor: University of Michigan Press, pp.105-121.

Van Horne, James C. (1985), Of Financial Innovations and Excesses, in: Journal of Finance, Vol.40, No.3, pp.621-631.

Wallich, Henry C. (1982), Forces that Drive International Monetary Evolution, in: Werner Ehrlicher/Diethart B. Simmert (eds.), Geld- und Währungspolitik in der Bundesrepublik Deutschland, Supplement to Kredit und Kapital, No.7, Berlin: Duncker & Humblot, pp.19-32.

Weiner, Stuart E. (1992), The Changing Role of Reserve Requirements in Monetary Policy, in: Federal Reserve Bank of Kansas City Economic Review, No.4, pp.45-63.

Weizsäcker, Carl Christian von (1987), Inwieweit ist es notwendig, Kapitalmärkte zu regulieren?, in: Dieter Schneider (ed.), Kapitalmarkt und Finanzierung, Berlin: Duncker & Humblot, pp.71-83.

Wellink, Arnout (1994), Experience Gained with Monetary Policy Instruments in the Netherlands, in: Deutsche Bundesbank, Auszüge aus Presseartikeln, No.41, 13.6.1994, pp.6-15.

Willeke, Franz-Ulrich (1994), Ein Wettbewerbsmodell für Europas Geldverfassung, in: Wirtschaftsdienst, Vol.74, No.2, pp.78-82.

List of Figures

List of Tables

Printing: Weihert-Druck GmbH, Darmstadt
Binding: Buchbinderei Schäffer, Grünstadt

GPSR Compliance

The European Union's (EU) General Product Safety Regulation (GPSR) is a set of rules that requires consumer products to be safe and our obligations to ensure this.

If you have any concerns about our products, you can contact us on ProductSafety@springernature.com

In case Publisher is established outside the EU, the EU authorized representative is:

Springer Nature Customer Service Center GmbH
Europaplatz 3
69115 Heidelberg, Germany

Batch number: 10682215

Printed by Printforce, the Netherlands